GW00985381

THE POWELLS IN ESSEX
AND THEIR LONDON
ANCESTORS

David Powell

b. 1695, d. 1784.

THE POWELLS IN ESSEX AND THEIR LONDON ANCESTORS

BY

RICHARD MORRIS, OBE
Verderer of Epping Forest

LOUGHTON
THE LOUGHTON AND DISTRICT HISTORICAL SOCIETY
2002

© Richard Morris 2002

ISBN 0954 231 42 2

Published in 2002 by the Loughton and District Historical Society
and available from Forest Villa, Staples Road, Loughton, Essex, IG10 1 HP

All rights reserved. No part of this publication may be reproduced,
stored in a retrieval system, or transmitted, in any form or by any means,
electronic, mechanical, photocopying, recording or otherwise without the prior
permission of the author and the Loughton and District Historical Society

Production and Index by
Ted Martin
Theydon Bois
Essex CM16 7JX

Jacket design, typesetting and reproduction by
Artform
Little Tew, Oxfordshire OX7 4JH

Printed in Great Britain by
The Lavenham Press
Lavenham, Suffolk

Contents

Illustrations

Introduction

The principal purpose of this memoir is to record the contributions made by a particular branch of the Powell family to the arts and the community during the eighteenth and nineteenth centuries. It has to be said that the philanthropic activities of the persons involved were based on the success of David Powell, who came to London from Suffolk in 1712, to be apprenticed as a salter, and who subsequently developed a substantial business as a merchant in the City of London. Later generations joined the family firm and widened its merchanting interests.

I have limited my researches to those members of David Powell's family who lived in the City of London and a few miles east at Homerton, Clapton and Tottenham, and to their descendants who moved further east, across the River Lea, into Essex. It is interesting that in the eighteenth century their houses in Homerton and Clapton were described as their 'country houses', with the mansions in the City as their 'town houses'.

If the contributions of members of the family towards the community were, in the main, confined to London and eastwards into Essex, the involvement in the arts was on a national basis. David Thomas Powell (1771-1848) devoted his life to researching the history and architecture of parish churches and manor houses throughout England and Wales, and many of his delightful watercolour sketches remain in the national collection at the British Library and at some county and local institutions. His reputation as an antiquarian of some standing appears only to have developed after his death, with the sale of many of his manuscripts, although he was related to a Keeper of the manuscripts at the British Museum, who on occasion sought his advice.

In 1834 James Powell purchased the glassworks at Whitefriars in the City of London to add to his wine merchant's business. What led him to do this at a time when other glassworks in London were closing, due to competition, is still a slight mystery, apart from his comment that he did so 'in order that his three sons should have sufficient occupation'. However, the second half of the nineteenth century and early part of the twentieth saw James Powell & Sons, or Whitefriars as it became known, at the zenith of its reputation as a maker of stained glass windows. Following the sad demise of the glassworks in 1980, the Museum of London acquired a major archive of the glasswork's products and records, and in 1995 published an

1

extensive volume on the history of the glassworks. In this short memoir the intention is only to mention briefly those members of the Powell family who made major contributions to the factory, and to refer to some of the churches in Essex where examples of Whitefriars glass can be found.

It was only during my research into David Powell's descendants that I came to appreciate the involvement of so many of the family in charities for the poor and the sick. For almost 200 years Powells took a leading role in the founding and management of St Luke's Hospital for 'poor lunatics'. This is still recognised today with the portrait of John Clark Powell hanging in the entrance hall of St Luke's-Woodside Hospital at Muswell Hill. The Rev David Thomas Powell's legacy to the London Hospital, part of which was used to build a new Medical College at the hospital, may have caused some friction in the family at the time of his death, but remains as an example of Christian charity. Nathanael Powell, as we shall see, contributed much to the development of King's College Hospital.

Several members of the Powell family entered the Church. One, Edmund Nathanael, became a bishop, but owing to ill health his tenure in this role was short lived. The Victorian era saw churchgoing as a part of family life and Nathanael Powell, Edmund's father, was a churchwarden of his parish church for 36 years. The church is, of course, often associated with education, and the Powells played their part, both financially and in the management of the local National Schools and some public schools.

In writing this memoir I have, where possible, given some details of the history of the houses and estates that the Powells acquired in east London and Essex, that may be of interest to the local historian.

I am most grateful to Dr Audrey Baker, the great granddaughter of Nathanael Powell, for her interest in the book, permission to quote from Nathanael Powell's memoir of his early life and to reproduce sketches of members of the family.

My researches have led me to both national and local sources of information. Edgar Powell's genealogy of the family, published in 1891, has been a prime source for the earlier years, and copies can be found in the British Library and at the Guildhall Library in the City of London. I am grateful to Rita Read, the archivist at the London Borough of Haringey, who was able to provide information on the life of Thomas Powell and his son David during their time at The Chestnuts in Tottenham. My thanks go also to David Mander, the archivist for the London Borough of Hackney, for his assistance in researching the life of the Powells at Homerton and Clapton.

The Museum and Archives at the Royal London Hospital were able to add to the details of David Thomas Powell's legacy to the hospital. My thanks are due to Sylvia Mannering at St Luke's-Woodside Hospital for the assistance given in 'discovering' the extent of the Powells' involvement at that hospital. The principal source for the chapter on Nathanael Powell and his family has been the six volumes of the family scrapbooks that are now held at the Vestry House Museum in Walthamstow. My thanks are due to Miss Jo Parker, the archivist at the London Borough of Waltham Forest, for her help during the several visits made to examine the scrapbooks.

The Essex Record Office has been able to provide information on the houses and estates of the Powells at Loughton and Theydon Bois. I am also most grateful to John Stradling, of the local studies section at the Loughton Branch of Essex County Libraries, for his patience in responding to many questions and for allowing me access to old records and maps.

The watercolour sketches by David Thomas Powell (Plates 5, 6, 7, 8, 9, 10, 11, 12, 13, 14, 15, 16, 17, 19, 20, 21, 23, 24, 25) have been reproduced by the kind permission of The British Library. The photograph of Grove House, Walthamstow (page 58) has been reproduced by the kind permission of the Vestry House Museum, London Borough of Waltham Forest.

This memoir could not have been published without the support of the Loughton and District Historical Society, and in particular Chris Pond and Ted Martin to whom I am grateful.

On the south wall of All Saints Church, at Hawstead in Suffolk, there is a small marble plaque, which was installed by the descendants of John Powell. It quotes the end of a letter that he wrote to his son David on 3 May 1724:

I conclude all with hearty prayer for God Allmighty's Blissings one you all and good wishes for yor good success in all yor undertakings, which good God if you take care to serve in your family and elcewhere as you ought, you need not fear His care for you, and it will intaile his Blissing one all yor posterity, wch still I heartily pray for as I ought being yor indulging Father.

RICHARD MORRIS
Loughton, July 2002

1

Merchants in London

In tracing the history of the branch of the Powell family that came to live in London and Essex, and who were to contribute much to the community, as well as establishing substantial business interests, we need first to refer to their origins in Suffolk.

In about 1661–62 Bridget, the wife of David Powell, gave birth to a son, John, at Barton Mills in Suffolk. By 1687 we find that John Powell had moved to Hawstead, and by 1689 he had married and was living at a farm, which he held under Mr Francis Hammond, Citizen and Salter of London. The farmhouse and buildings, known as Hammond's Farm (Plate 1), lay a little above the hamlet called Pinford End. Six sons and one daughter were born to John and his wife Katharine. In June 1712, John took his second son, David, then just 17 up to London, where he was bound apprentice to Mr Francis Hammond as a salter. Of the other five sons, Charles and Frederick went later to London to seek their fortunes. John, Henry and William remained in Suffolk, with Henry eventually succeeding his father at Hammond's Farm.

David Powell (1695-1784)

When John Powell returned to Hawstead from taking his son David to London, he immediately wrote a letter to his son that is dated 25 June 1712:

As soon as I was well got home I could not forbear writing to inquire of your welfare and how you fear in all things, here was some little sorrow for your departure but I hope that will be turned into joy when we hear you are well and easy. In order to which forget not, but remember thy Creator now in the days of your youth, who has promised he will never forget those that remember him and depend on him, therefore if sinners entice you, do not consent. As for your shirts we think not to send them while we whither you stay or not, and then you shall want nothing that is necessary.

I came to Poslingford from London where I stayed and brought your cousin Bridget home with me. You had best buy some coarse apron.

This is all from your loving Father.

John Powell.

Pray ye first opportunity let me have a line or two from you.

For David Powell.
Attention Mr Middleton near the Dial in Broad Street.
London.[1]

The books of the Salters' Company in London record that:

David Powell, son of John Powell of Hawstead, Suffolk, bound apprentice to Francis Hammond 5 September 1712. [He was probably on trial for the first three months after his arrival in London.] Turned over to Charles Middleton and by his widow to James Baden 18 April 1716. Sworn and made free 16 March 1720.

A few months after David Powell had completed his apprenticeship his father, in a letter dated 9 August 1720, gave thanks for the harvest of that year, although it had been a wet season. He also asks if David and his brother Charles could come to Hawstead and help with the harvest. John Powell ends this letter by giving some advice to his son, which judging by his subsequent success, he took to heart:

My humble servis to Mr Baden and ye rest. My advice is to save what money you can honestly; now in your time while youth lasts. Business may fall off, or sick or lame days may come, however old age will, and any make a man unfit for action. Consider it is a great deal you must disburse in a year for mere necessities.

In the parish accounts at Hawstead, John Powell's name appears as churchwarden. He died there on 16 June 1725 aged about 64 years. His tombstone stands in the churchyard. In 1884 the descendants of John Powell installed a stained glass window in his memory in All Saints Church, Hawstead (Plates 2 and 3). The inscription at the base of the window reads:

This window to the memory of John Powell of Hawstead, born 1661, died 16 June 1725. The gift of descendants in grateful recognition of prayers he was wont to make for his children and their posterity, is presented as a thankoffering to God for the many blessings vouchsafed in answer thereto. The effectual fervent prayer of a righteous man availeth much.

On Saturday, 27 April 1723, David Powell had married, at St Andrews Church, Enfield, Susannah, daughter and co-heiress of Edward Thistlethwayte, of the Close, Salisbury, who had married a cousin of James Baden. The Thistlethwaytes and Badens had entered into partnership as exchange brokers and merchants. The Badens were members of the Mercers Company, one of the oldest and wealthiest City Livery companies, and it may have been one of the reasons why many members of the Powell family became connected with the Company and took an active part in it during the nineteenth and twentieth centuries

After their marriage, David and his wife Susannah lived at Crown Court, Broad Street, in the City of London, until they moved four miles east to Clapton, to a property called Byland House at 185 Lower Clapton Road, which stood on the left of the high road from London, just before Clapton Pond. In the yard behind the house was a lead cistern with the initials DSP, meaning David and Susannah Powell, and the date 1761 on it, which is probably the year when they came to Clapton. David bought the freehold of Byland House in 1783. In 1766 David purchased the estate of Wattisfield

David Powell (1725–1810)

Hall, Suffolk, and became the Lord of the Manor. He had already, 10 years earlier, purchased a property at Walsham-le-Willows.

David and Susannah had seven children, all sons, two of whom died in infancy and one who died at the young age of just less than seven years. As we shall see, the surviving sons followed their father into the family business and expanded it. In 1784 David Powell died at Clapton at the age of 89, and was buried in the churchyard of St John's, Hackney. From a statement of accounts made by his son Baden, who was acting as executor, it appears that the total value of his estate, after all debts were paid, amounted to £65,475. David's will provided for the residue of his personal estate to be divided equally between his four surviving sons: Baden, David, James and Thomas. However, prior to his death, he had instructed his four sons to draw lots as to which should be given the freehold and copyhold estates at Wattisfield and Walsham-le-Willows in Suffolk. The estates were valued at £5,250 and this sum was to be paid into the personal estate by whoever inherited title to the property, to be divided between the four sons as part of the residue. Baden Powell was successful in drawing the lot to inherit the freehold and copyhold of the estates, and formal title was transferred to him. Each of the grandchildren, and there were many, received £500.

David Powell (1725-1810)

David, the eldest surviving son of David and Susannah, was born on 13 December 1725. He was baptised at the church of St Peter-le-Poor in Threadneedle Street, as were all his brothers. However, the church no longer exists. In 1736 we find him at the Rev Dr Dorman's school at Kensington, to which his brothers also went. He was a person of considerable ability, which showed itself early and caused his uncle, Thomas Baden, to advise a university education for the boy. He evidently employed his time well at Dr Dorman's school, and the following well-written note at the age of 10 to his mother is interesting:

Mary tells me you was much frighted last night a going home. I shall be very uneasy till I know how you do; and how my dear father got to town. I beg Madam you will write me word as soon as ever this comes to hand. My Duty to my father.

I am your most Dutiful and obliged son.

David Powell.

Kensington.
May 20, 1736

My master and mistress present their humble service and they too are very impatient to know how you do.

Laetitia Powell (1741–1801)

The note is addressed on the back to Mrs Susannah Powell in Crown Court, Broad Street, behind the Royal Exchange. At that date, during the Walpole administration, travelling was dangerous and rioting serious and frequent in London, which may explain the boy's anxiety.[2]

In July 1741 David was bound apprentice to Mr James Whitchurch, junior, merchant, London. In the bond it is stated that the hours of work were to be from 9 till 2, and from 3 till he obtained leave from Mr Whitchurch to go. In 1760 he went into partnership with his brother, Thomas, the capital of the firm being £6,000, of which David owned three-quarters, and Thomas one-quarter. In 1766 the capital was increased to £9,000, each partner owning a half-share. In 1785 John Clark Powell, David's eldest son, was taken into the firm as a partner, the capital then being £12,000, of which the two seniors held £5,000 each and John Clark Powell £2,000.

In *Lowndes' Directory* of 1787, the family firms are given:

Powell, David and Thomas, merchants, 4 Little St Helens.
Powell, Baden and James, merchants, 3 Crown Court, Broad Street.

In 1761, at the age of 35 years, David was married at St Botolph's, Bishopsgate, to Laetitia, daughter and heiress of John Clark of Bishopsgate Street. They lived at Homerton and at Little St Helen's where was also the counting house of the firm. David and Laetitia had fourteen children, of whom four did not survive infancy, leaving five sons and five daughters.

In 1794 David Powell became Treasurer of St Luke's Hospital, London, a post in which he was followed by other members of the family.

In January 1810 David died at Homerton at the age of 84. He was buried in the tomb of his father in the churchyard at Hackney. David's career as a London merchant, dealing largely with Italy, was no doubt very successful and from accounts of his executors it appears that he owned freeholds in various places valued at over £35,000, and government and other public securities valued at over £216,000.

Under his will he left to his eldest son, John Clark Powell, all the estates in Horton Kirby, Farningham and Swanscombe in Kent. Property in Gracechurch Street and Eastcheap in the City of London also went to him. To his son Baden he left property in Fenchurch Street, Star Alley and Mark Lane. His son Harry received the Nockhall estate at Swanscombe. His son James received three houses at Homerton as Laetitia, David's wife, had pre-deceased him. The second eldest son, David, received the estate at Alkerden or Combe at Swanscombe. He had already received a considerable estate at Loughton from one of father's brothers who had died in 1802. David's life and tragic death by a strike of lightning are described in Chapter 4. The four grandchildren received £750 each.

After David Powell's death his family moved from Homerton to Clapton, to a house now pulled down but which stood near the Pond, and between the main street and what is now Powell Road. This house continued to be where John Clark Powell lived until his death in 1847 and afterwards of his two unmarried sisters, who survived him.

Baden Powell (1731-1802)

The second eldest surviving son of David and Susannah Powell was Baden Powell, who was born in Crown Court, Broad Street, on 15 March 1731. He joined the family firm and went into partnership with his younger brother James. As we have seen, he was legatee of all his father's landed property. It is not clear whether he moved from the City of London to Byland House, Clapton, with his father in about 1761 or had a separate property in that part of Middlesex. However, in 1772 he moved to Bench House, Loughton, some eight miles further north-east in Essex, where he lived until his death in 1802. This part of his life is described in Chapter 4 which deals with the Powells in Loughton.

Thomas Powell (1735-1820)

The third surviving son of David and Susannah Powell was Thomas, who was born at Crown Court on 19 August 1735. As with his other brothers, he went into the family business, this time with his brother David, although initially as the junior partner. In May 1770 he married Catharine Smith who was the daughter of Dr Smith of St Petersburg, physician to the Empress Catherine of Russia. Thomas became known as an author of some plays and poems of sufficient merit that a collection remains today in the National Library of Wales.[3] Thomas and Catharine may have lived for a short while at Buckingham Street in the Strand before moving to Tottenham. This could account for the baptism of their children in the Private Chapel at Somerset House. Their life at Tottenham is described more fully in Chapter 2.

James Powell (1737-1824)

The Powell's played a prominent part in the history of Clapton in East London but it is difficult to establish who purchased various properties in the district, and who lived in them in the latter part of the eighteenth century. The youngest son of David and Susannah Powell, was James, who was born in July 1737 and, as we have seen, he went into partnership in business with his brother Baden. In November 1775 he married Anne Cornthwaite, daughter of the Rev Thomas Cornthwaite, who was vicar of Hackney for 46 years. Where James Powell actually lived in Clapton is not clear but it was in a house described as 'the Freehold Mansion House in the occupation of James Powell situated near the Pond at Clapton in the parish of St John's Hackney'. In a plan of 1799 James Powell's name is against a house just south-west of the Pond near where Byland House stood. It has been suggested that, on the death of David Powell the elder, in 1784, his son and heir David conveyed Byland House to his brother James. It was James Powell who purchased nearly all the properties of which the Powell estate in Hackney has consisted.[4]

In 1799 James Powell bought the Clapton House estate of about 22 acres. This included Clapton House, although he never lived there. This building was a fine mansion in which various members of the family lived as tenants. The origins of Clapton House go back to at least the seventeenth century when it was assessed for 14 hearths and Bishop Wood lived there. It was called the bishop's mansion for over a century, Lizhards or Leezhards in 1749, and Clapton House in 1799. Improvements 'nearly equal to rebuilding' were made for the lessee Israel Levin Salomons. Features included a marble paved hall, a library, and in the five acres of pleasure grounds, a structure resembling an orangery or banqueting room. Powell bought further property in the area including the Hackney Water Works and the Corn Mills. On the death of his brother Baden in 1802 he inherited the Manor of Wattisfield in Suffolk and he purchased Newick Park in Sussex. James died in 1824 and was buried in the family grave at Hackney. A great deal of the Clapton estate he left to his two daughters, one of whom, Hester, had married her cousin Baden in 1795. His other property went to his son Thomas Baden Powell, a Fellow of Oriel College, Oxford, and Rector of Newick. This son married Sarah Louisa, daughter of Nathanael Cotton, Rector of Thornby, Northants.

In 1840 the Rev T B Powell gave a cottage and land called the Strawberry garden, opposite Clapton House, as a site for St James's Church. The new church was financed by the Hackney church building committee as a chapel of ease. It was described as 'commodious and handsome, crucifix in form, much broken in parts, producing great variety and picturesque effect'. Building started on 25 July (St James's Day) 1840 and finished in October 1841. The church could seat 1,050 persons, although this was later reduced to 900. James Cotton Powell was the first incumbent, followed by his cousin George Powell and George's nephew George Powell Irby.

James Powell (1774–1840)

James Powell (1774-1840)

A son of David and Laetitia Powell who merits a separate mention is James, who was born at Homerton in October 1774. He went into partnership with John Powell of Millman Street as a wine merchant, and they ran the business from 60 Carey Street, behind the Law Courts, which also served as the family's 'town house'. The house was built in 1731–32 for Richard Foley, an MP and bencher of Lincoln's Inn, and is today the London residence of the President of the Law Society (Plate 4). The house has three storeys and is built of red brick. The interior remains an excellent example of an early Georgian business and dwelling-house. In Powell's time there was a small walled garden but this was destroyed when an extension to the house was built in 1929-30. At that time, when the foundations were dug, the builders discovered a 12m tunnel, 2m high, and 1m wide, probably cut in the early nineteenth century. The tunnel, which had niches for candles and small pulley wheels, perhaps for a bell pull, runs from a vault under the garden with two turns towards Star Yard, possibly connecting with other tunnels. This, no doubt, was where the wine was stored.

In 1834 Powell purchased the glassworks at Whitefriars on the north bank of the River Thames off Fleet Street. The Powell family were to remain involved with the glassworks until its closure in 1980. The involvement of James and his descendants in the glassworks is described in Chapter 8.

In January 1807 James married Catharine, daughter of Nathanael Cotton, Rector of Thornby, Northants. They had eight children, four sons and four daughters, and several of the sons became partners in the Whitefriars firm. James and Catharine lived for a time at Shore Place in Hackney but in 1839 James took a lease on Clapton House from his cousin the Rev Thomas Baden Powell. James was followed at Clapton House by his sons James Cotton Powell and Arthur who worked at Whitefriars. Clapton House was demolished in 1885 to make way for Thistlethwaite Road. A number of roads in the area now bear the names of Suffolk villages with which the Powells were associated. The neighbouring Byland House served as a vicarage for the second and third incumbents of St James's, both of them related to the Rev Thomas Baden Powell. The house was sold to the local council in 1932 and demolished to make way for council housing.[5]

Baden Powell (1767-1844)

Mention has already been made of Baden Powell who received some property from the estate of his father, David Powell, and who had also married his cousin, Hester. Born at Little St Helens in November 1767 he followed a successful business career in the City and owned estates at Langton and Speldhurst in Kent. He became High Sheriff of Kent and Master of the Mercers' Company. He had four children, the eldest of whom, Baden, was to become a Fellow of the Royal Society and Savilian Professor of Geometry at Oxford University. This branch of the Powell family lived mainly in Kent. However, there is a link with Essex in that the sixth son of Professor Baden Powell and his third wife, Henrietta, was Robert Smyth Baden Powell, the founder of the Scout movement, who when created a peer took the title Baron Baden-Powell of Gilwell in Essex. Gilwell was acquired for the Scout movement in 1919 and Robert Baden Powell oversaw the purchase and development of the site. Although he visited Gilwell on many occasions, he never lived there. Today it is the headquarters of the Scout movement and an international camping site.

REFERENCES

1. Powell, E, *Pedigree of the Family of Powell* (1891), is the source for much of this chapter.
2. Powell, E, *Pedigree of the Family of Powell* (revised edition, 1926).
3. National Library of Wales, Cwrtmawr MSS 427-442.
4. Hackney Archives, Bagust Collection, vol 13A.
5. *Victoria History of the County of Middlesex*, vol x, p 86.

2

'The Chestnuts', Tottenham

Thomas Powell moved to Tottenham shortly after his marriage to Catharine Smith in 1770. In July 1773 he was given leave to enclose a piece of waste in front of his house containing from north to south 200 feet and from east to west 30 feet, on paying annually 10s 6d to the churchwardens for the benefit of the poor forever.[1] In April 1776 he was given leave to enclose a part of the waste in the west front of his house where some chestnut trees stood, containing 65 feet from north to south and 19 feet from east to west; he and his heirs paying annually forever to the churchwardens and overseers of the poor 5 shillings. Only a month later Thomas Powell was given permission to enclose the remaining waste in the front of his house, this time paying annually 16 shillings for the use of the poor.[2]

The Chestnuts, as the house was called, was to be the home of Thomas Powell's family for almost 80 years, until the death of his son David Thomas Powell in 1848. The house stood at the corner of Tottenham High Road and Chestnut Road, where today is Tottenham Police Station. It was a large house enclosed in a high brick wall and was built by Will Latimer of Warwick. It had a flight of stone steps to the front door, and a window in the hall on each side of the door.[3] The garden was well known for its profusion of violets. At the time of its demolition in about 1860 it was described as commanding an open view over the Essex hills.[4] The house and garden occupied just over two acres but in addition another nine acres of meadow was later acquired, together with three cottages.[5]

Thomas and Catharine Powell's first child was born on 29 January 1771. This was David Thomas Powell. He was baptised on 25 February in the Private Chapel of Somerset House. Baptisms, marriages and burials took place in this chapel until it was demolished in 1776. David Thomas Powell was to become an antiquary of considerable renown. However, in 1789, the year of the French Revolution, he joined the army and was gazetted as an Ensign in the 17th Regiment of Foot. In 1791 he was a Lieutenant in the 11th Dragoons, but in 1795 he left the army. Two years later he became an undergraduate at Magdalen College, Oxford, where he read law. On leaving university he entered the Anglican Church and was subsequently appointed curate of Ashurst, but it does not appear that he ever became the incumbent of any parish.

No record exists of his earlier education but drawing and painting no doubt featured as, by 1789, at the age of 17½ years, he was making sketches in watercolour of buildings in Essex. One of the first was of Woolston Hall, a manor house near Chigwell, occupied for several centuries by the Scott family. The drawing (Plate 5) possibly lacks a little in character but this may be due to Powell's draughtsman's-like approach to sketching buildings. He was fortunate that he inherited considerable wealth from his father and, as a result, his interest in the topographical history of England and Wales became a full-time occupation, and over a period of nearly 50 years he visited 40 counties, making sketches in watercolours of the principal buildings in many villages, mainly churches, and writing short notes on the history of the village, churches and locally important families. A fuller appreciation of this academic side of his life is given in the next chapter.

The Chestnuts in Tottenham became the repository for a mass of information gathered by David Thomas Powell and this included a considerable library of books on subjects ranging from history, heraldry and architecture to philosophy, poetry and the sciences. He also collected paintings, prints and miniatures. All these items were carefully recorded in a catalogue, which the auctioneer found of great assistance when preparing the sale of the contents of the house following Powell's death in June 1848. The collection has been widely dispersed but a substantial number of manuscripts have survived, including Powell's own catalogues, and are listed in Appendix B.

Powell's travels around the counties were probably made on horseback. On occasions he describes the route taken, as in his journey on Tuesday, 30 October (no date is given but most likely to have been 1789) when he rode out from Tottenham to Essex, no doubt calling on his uncle Baden Powell at Bench House, Loughton:

Left Tottenham about 10, by marshes [to] Chingford, across [Epping] Forest by Loughton, arrived at Epping, noticing the instruments [earthworks] said to have been thrown up by Queen Boadicea, opposite the newly erected gamekeepers lodge. Having baited my horse I rode on towards Harlow and noticed Latton Priory situated on a small eminence at a disused farm. The road in a very beautiful sequestered situation. Instead of going through Harlow I struck off at [the] Moreton road near a private house of a Mr Fothergill lately fitted up with a quantity of stained glass windows which of course drew me to it. [Here he describes some of the windows.] Flemish Arms and one shield of sixteen quarters with Garter and coronet of Dudley, Earl of Leicester.[6]

The note ends somewhat abruptly here, so that we do not know whether Powell returned to Tottenham that afternoon or stayed overnight at a local inn or house. His reference to the earthworks near Epping is to Ambresbury Banks, which today are considered to be of early Iron Age origin and not to have involved Boadicea or any of her battles.

On another visit to Loughton in January 1795, where he sketched the church of St Nicholas and Loughton Hall, Powell provides us with carefully drawn maps of his outward and return routes, noting the main landmarks, including lock houses [on the River Lea], inns, houses (including 'my uncle's') and churches.

A contemporary of Powell at Tottenham has suggested that:

He was going to be married, and on the morning of the day the wedding was to take place, he received a message from the lady saying she had altered her mind. From then until his death he never let a woman enter his house, and never went out, excepting now and then when he preached at St Paul's Cathedral. He had a large garden, with a bathroom and swimming bath in the middle of the lawn, all beautifully tiled, at the back was a fish pond and meadow. The last time I saw him he was looking over the high brick wall with a blanket over his shoulders. He used to give dinner parties to his gentlemen friends; everything was prepared and sent down with waiters from London.[7]

If the above report is to be considered accurate, it can only be assumed that Powell's 'disappointment' must have occurred in the later years of his life, bearing in mind that he was to visit and write topographical notes on 40 counties.

That Powell became somewhat eccentric as old age approached is more likely. This is confirmed by Albert Hall, who recalled that when funds were being raised to fight an outbreak of cholera, his father and friends visited, among others, an eccentric old gentleman residing at The Chestnuts. Somehow the old gentleman got wind of their intended call, and hid himself in his hayloft to avoid them. They nevertheless persevered in their errand, and went their way rejoicing with a guinea wrung from the 'miser'. Hall repeats the story that Powell as a young man, having a university education, he had been the gayest of gay, the observed of all observed, but a cruel disappointment had converted him into an inveterate recluse.[8]

Powell employed a Mr Stockley as his personal attendant and manager of his affairs. Mr Stockley's name appears as a witness to a letter dated 20 March 1833 from Powell to the surveyor of the Assessed Taxes, in which he advises that previous to the fifth of April next 1833 the number of windows in his house and outhouses will be reduced to the number of 22, and not that in the last survey he made; three windows in the stable were charged which stable was not in Mr Powell's occupation on 20 March 1833.[9] This not only tells us something about the man but also indicates the size of his house.

David Thomas Powell died at The Chestnuts on 9 June 1848. A report in a local newspaper of his death was somewhat unfairly headed 'Death of a Miser at Tottenham', and reported that:

During the last few days much conversation and surprise have prevailed among the inhabitants of Tottenham in consequence of the death of the Rev. David Thomas Powell, a minister of the Church of England, who was highly connected, and who it was supposed from his penurious habits, was far from being in good circumstances. He lived near the High Cross, and his attendant was a little boy, who was the only person who had any control over him. He avoided all company. He died on 9th June of the present month, upon which his relatives made a search for his will. Sergeant Butcher of the 'N' Division, and a solicitor proceeded to the house. They entered the room which he occupied, but they were unable to remain in it from the effluvium that prevailed there, and they were obliged to have it fumigated before they were able to look for his will. This was discovered, upon which it was ascertained that his real and personal property amounted to between £50,000 and £60,000. Of this he had bequeathed £1,000 to the boy who attended upon him, £600 to his [the boy's] brother, a legacy to each of his executors [William and Walter Robinson] and above £30,000 to the London Hospital, having disinherited the whole of his relatives. The landed property, which is situated in Tottenham, is estimated at £10,000 value, the right to which, it is stated, will be disputed by Sir Henry Martin who is the heir at law to the deceased.[10]

The newspaper report must be treated as being economical with the facts. Powell, as we have seen, never married and most if not all of his relations were well off. As a man of the church he was following his Christian principles in providing first for the sick and poor. His reputation is as a miser, but his lasting testament lies in his work as an antiquary and the record of this remains in national and local libraries and museums.

The newspaper report refers to the residue of his estate being left to the London Hospital. It was, however, four years before the Hospital received any funds from this bequest. Sir Henry Martin, the third baronet, and Powell's nephew, contested the terms of the will on the grounds of 'sufficient insanity of the Testator'. The London Hospital also took legal advice from 'the ablest counsel' as to their right, as a charity, to receive the real estate part of Powell's will. Counsel's opinion was that the Hospital was not exempt from the Statute of Mortmain and that therefore the Governors of the Hospital could not receive the residue of the real estate. It had been estimated that the personal estate under Powell's will was valued at £32,000 and the real estate £10,000.

Powell's executors, William Robinson from White Hart Lane and Walter Robinson from Risborough in Buckinghamshire, decided to file a Bill in Chancery to obtain the direction of the court in the administration of the estate. There followed a period of almost four years before the court heard the case. Documents proving who were the heir at law and next of kin were lost. The solicitor acting for the executors was involved in a serious accident and ultimately had to be replaced. However, in July 1852 the Vice-Chancellor of the Court of Chancery gave his judgment. He found against Sir Henry Martin on the main issue of insanity and gave immediate authority for the transfer of £27,000 to the London Hospital. He also agreed that the bank stock and London Assurance shares could be bequeathed to a charity, but reserved his judgment on the point, as a similar case had recently gone to appeal. However, two years later the Hospital received another £3,080 in this respect. Sir Henry Martin also tried to argue that the Hospital had no entitlement to any of the estate as the annual income of the Hospital already exceeded the £4,000 laid down in its Charter. The Vice-Chancellor advised that this was a matter that could only be raised by the Attorney-General on behalf of the Crown and, as they were already a party to the suit and had no objection to the court's award, he overruled the claim.

There then only remained the issue of the proportion of debts and legacies that should be borne by the real estate, of which the heir at law was the inheritor, and which had been paid in the first instance out of the personal estate. This was resolved by an agreement under seal between the executors, the London Hospital and Sir Henry Martin.[11]

At about the time that the first steps were being taken to resolve the contested will in the courts, the House Committee of the London Hospital had in 1851 received a request from the Medical College for assistance in the maintenance of the College. The medical school had been founded in 1785 as a private venture on the part of the staff. The Hospital had provided the plot of ground on which the College had been built at the north-east corner of the Hospital but had provided no financial assistance. The House Committee received the proposal sympathetically but decided not to provide any pecuniary assistance at that time, but would not lose sight of the subject and should an opportunity arise they would provide them with increased and improved accommodation.

Almost two years later, when the funds from Powell's bequest had been received, the Hospital decided to apply part of the legacy to the building of a new Medical College. The Committee decided that the old buildings would be given up for the general purposes of the Hospital and replaced by one on a larger scale to be erected by the Governors on the south-west corner of the Hospital grounds. The estimated cost was £6,300. So a new Medical College was built and formally opened on 2 October 1854, when John Davies, Esq, a past officer, acting for the Treasurer, and Sir Edward North Buxton delivered the keys granting the tenancy of the new College to the medical and surgical staff. The building still exists in Turner Street, albeit extended and modernised on several occasions.[12]

Powell was buried in the churchyard of St Nicholas Church, Loughton, with his brother Henry alongside him. Henry had been born on 13 May 1774 but had only survived for just short of three years. The choice of the churchyard at Loughton is slightly puzzling. His uncle Baden had lived in the village from 1772 until his death in 1802 but was buried at St John's, Hackney. However, his nephew, David, who predeceased him in 1832, also lived at Loughton and is buried nearby in the churchyard.

In June 1772 a sister, Catharine, had been born who, like her brothers David Thomas and Henry, had been baptised in the Private Chapel at Somerset House. On 23 June 1792 Catharine had married Sir Henry Martin, second baronet, at Tottenham Church. They had three children, one of whom, Henry, died in infancy in 1794, and lies buried in St Nicholas churchyard, Loughton, together with his grandfather, the first baronet, Sir Henry Martin, who also died in 1794. Why Sir Henry Martin, together with his wife who died in 1808, should be buried in Loughton has puzzled local historians for many years. The first baronet lived at Lockynge in Berkshire. He had been a Member of Parliament for Southampton, Comptroller of His Majesty's Navy and an Elder Brother of Trinity House. His only connection with Loughton was that his son had married Catharine Powell.

Interest in the Martin family does not lie principally with Sir Henry, but with his daughter Sarah Catherine, who also lies buried in the same vault, with her parents and nephew. Sarah Catherine was born in January 1768 and died in December 1826. She was the author of the universally popular story of *Old Mother Hubbard*.[13] It is now impossible to read the inscriptions on the sides of the Martin tomb and the railings that once surrounded the tomb have been removed. The tomb lies between David Thomas Powell and his brother, Henry, and the tomb of David Powell and his two wives, Mary and Grizell. Although now surrounded by a council estate, an architecturally less than prestigious college and the M11, Loughton churchyard was always remarked on by nineteenth century commentators as a sylvan and peaceful site overlooking the Roding.

Thomas Powell's first wife, Catharine, died in 1780. In 1786 Thomas married Clarissa Madden. One son, Henry Wayland, was born of this marriage in 1787. Henry Wayland Powell served in the Grenadier Guards and saw action at Waterloo. He died in 1840. His mother came from a distinguished family of public servants. Mrs Clarissa Powell lived at The Chestnuts in Tottenham from the time of her marriage, until shortly after her husband's death in 1820. In 1804 she was involved in the setting up of the first local savings bank specifically for the benefit of the lower classes. It was called the Charitable Bank and had the sole and express object of providing a safe and profitable place of deposit for the savings of the industrious poor, labourers, servants and others.

This savings bank was for many years under the direction and management of Mrs Powell. She was assisted in her laudable undertaking by a treasurer. All purchases of stock made from the deposits were placed in the names of the trustees. In 1818 there was £2,000 stock in 5% gilts besides a balance in the hands of the treasurer. The deposits were principally derived from servants and poor people who either had small sums bequeathed to them, or from savings of their wages. Some of them made deposits as small as seven shillings in a quarter, but in one instance, shortly after the bank was established, a nurse placed £160 of her savings in the bank. The whole of the accounts were under the management of Mrs Powell, into whose hands the deposits were paid and who paid the interest on the first Monday in every month to those who wished to have it. The bank was taken over by the Post office in 1865 when deposits amounted to £19,396.[14]

Clarissa Powell died in 1847.

REFERENCES

1. Vestry Minute Book B, p 189.
2. Vestry Minute Book E, pp 5 and 271.
3. Fisk, F, *The History of Tottenham* (1923), p 224.
4. *Ibid,* p 225.
5. Rate Book 1843.
6. British Library Add MS 17460, f 60.
7. Couchman, J W, *Reminiscences of Tottenham* (1909).
8. Hall, Albert, *Seventy Two Years in Tottenham* (1899).
9. British Library Add MS 17460, f 59, on the back of a drawing.
10. Vestry House Museum, Powell Scrapbook, vol.1, f 18.
11. Royal London Hospital Archives, *House Committee Minutes 1848-1854,* LH/A/5/25-27.
12. Clark-Kennedy, A E, *The London,* vol 2 (1963).
13. *Essex Review*, vol xxv, pp 117 and 171.
14. Robinson, William, *History and Antiquities of Tottenham* (1840), p 281.

3

David Thomas Powell – Antiquary

We have seen that at an early age David Thomas Powell had started making watercolour sketches of churches and other buildings on journeys from his home at Tottenham, Middlesex. His interest in the history of the countryside and its buildings became a full-time occupation judging by the number of villages that he visited. While he does not rank among the highest of the county historians, his work provides a record of what the buildings he visited looked like at the end of the eighteenth and the first half of the nineteenth centuries. In many cases Powell had studied the history of a village before making a visit and subsequently compared his impression with that of an earlier historian.

Powell produced a portfolio of his writings and drawings for each of the counties that he visited, but out of the 40 counties visited, only 20 portfolios are known to survive, although there may be others in private collections. However, Powell did produce a single volume in which he summarised his findings in all the counties. This work survives and is entitled:

A Brief Account Of My Personal Visitations
Of A Great Number Of Places In England And Wales

By David Thomas Powell
Of Tottenham, Middlesex

In Course of Many Years
Containing very brief notices of what I drew or described,
That were most interesting to me or the most to my purpose.
Done as an imperfect reference to my large portfolio
Under the heads of the different counties.[1]

Appendix C lists the counties visited by Powell.

In addition to his topographical surveys, David Thomas Powell took a great interest in heraldry and produced a number of portfolios of drawings of the Arms of various families and orders of chivalry. In the latter respect the Arms of the Knights of the Order of St Michel and the Knights of the Golden Fleece are contained in three substantial volumes.[2] A portfolio of drawings of monuments in Westminster Abbey also survives.[3] Powell's knowledge of heraldry is recognised in correspondence between him and Sir Frederick Madden. Powell's father's second wife, Clarissa, was related to Sir Frederick and was probably his aunt. Sir Frederick Madden was 30 years younger than David Thomas Powell. From an early age he had also displayed a strong bias towards antiquarian and literary pursuits. He mastered Norman-French and Anglo-Saxon. In 1826 he was employed by the British Museum to assist in the preparation of the classified catalogue of printed books. In 1828 he was appointed as Assistant Keeper of manuscripts and in 1837 he became head of the Manuscripts Department. Two such kindred spirits as Frederick Madden and Powell corresponded on the interpretation and origin of various coats of arms and one can imagine them meeting at the British Museum.

One of the portfolios of drawings and descriptions of villages which still exists is that for the county of Essex.[4] David Thomas Powell's uncle, Baden Powell, had come to live in Essex in 1772, and his uncle's nephew David Powell had moved to Loughton from Walthamstow following Baden's death in 1802. The portfolio of Essex villages contains some 420 folios of which about half consist of drawings and brass rubbings, with the other half being descriptions of the villages and particular buildings. The link with his relations in south and south-west Essex makes it appropriate to quote some of Powell's descriptions and illustrations of places with which his relations were familiar.

Walthamstow

Walthamstow was but a short journey from Tottenham across the River Lea and marshes. Powell describes the village as lying between Wanstead, Woodford and the River Lea, and points out that the name is derived from *weald* meaning forest, *ham* a habitation or village and *stow* a place. He notes the early history of the village from the time of the Confessor and William the Conqueror. The interest of the Maynard family in one of the manors is made with the comment:

It is a very extensive manor known as Walthamstow Toni or High Hall. Courts were held at Toni Hall, a spacious brick house in Shernhall about a quarter mile south from the church.

A description of St Mary's Church follows together with three drawings, one of the exterior of the church and two of the monument to Lady Stanley Percy. (Plates 7 and 8).

Chingford

Adjoining Walthamstow, to the north, is Chingford, where Powell visited the old church of St Paul (it has now reverted to its earlier dedication of All Saints) which he describes as:

standing on the summit of one of those pretty gently rising hills whose line forms the western boundary of the county of Essex from Middlesex, commanding a fine view south to London, and a vast extent of marshland extending from Waltham to the River Thames watered by the River Lea. It is a sequestered village on the border of Epping Forest consisting of detached houses and cottages far removed from each other. The church stands alone, except for a large house at the east end, and on the other side [of] the road. It consists of a gabled nave divided from a side aisle on the south side only by four pointed arches on circular pillars with capitals of the time.

Powell continues with a full architectural description of the church in which in which he comments that the font is by far the oldest piece of work here to be found and seems a Saxon work composed of grey Sussex marble. 'The whole building is covered with a profusion of ivy which gives it a most picturesque appearance.'

There follow details of the principal monuments in the church including those for Robert Leigh and his family and Robert Rampston, the latter a great benefactor of several local parishes. Powell recites the delightful inscription, in verse form, to Robert Leigh's wife Marye:

> Marye the wife of Robert Leigh Esq
> Payes here the debt, that nature doth require
> Who lived a mirror for a Godly life
> And died a wonder, for a loving wife
> A body chaste, a virtuous mind
> A temperate tongue an humble heart
> Secret and wise, faithful and kind
> A friend to peace, a foe to strife
> A spotlesse Dame, a matchless wife
> Lie here her true anatomye
> And for her birth of gentletrie
> She Joslyne hight of Gourels Race
> Each tribe did give her equal Grace.

There are two watercolour drawings of the church, one of which is dated March 1802. There is a small colour drawing of windows in the chancel and a pencil drawing of what appears to be the font. Powell's watercolours of monuments are always very detailed and the one for John Leigh is no exception. On his journey from Tottenham, Powell would have passed Chingford Hall and in 1789 he made a watercolour sketch of the Hall, on the back of which is the inscription 'Chingford Hall in 1789. The manor house of the Manor of St Paul.' (See Plate 9.)

Powell adds a personal note at the end of this folio saying that the Rev Robert Lewis, 50 years Rector and 57 years joint lecturer of St John's, Hackney, deceased in his eighty-fifth year, on 27 December 1827. St John's, Hackney, was the Powell church for many years during which the family lived at Clapton. The Powell vault in the churchyard contains approximately 10 Powells.

Plate 1   Hammond's Farm, Hawstead, Suffolk, in 2002. The house goes back to the seventeenth century. David Powell lived there until he came to London in 1712.

Plate 2   All Saints Church, Hawstead, Suffolk.

Plate 3   The Powell memorial window in All Saints Church, Hawstead, Suffolk.

Plate 4   60 Carey Street, London. James Powell lived there and ran his wine merchants' business from the house in the early nineteenth century.

Plate 5   Woolston Hall, Chigwell, Essex, sketched by David Thomas Powell in 1789.

Plate 6   East Ham Church, Essex, sketched by David Thomas Powell in about 1800.

Plate 7 St Mary's Church, Walthamstow, Essex, sketched by David Thomas Powell in about 1795.

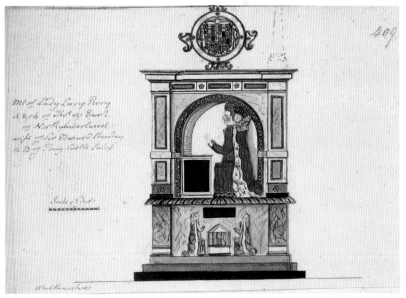

Plate 8 Lady Percy monument in St Mary's Church, Walthamstow, sketched by David Thomas Powell in about 1795.

Plate 9 Chingford Hall, Essex, sketched by David Thomas Powell in 1789.

Plate 10 Chingford Old Church, Essex, sketched by David Thomas Powell in 1802.

Plate 12 St Nicholas's Church, Loughton, sketched by David Thomas Powell in 1790. The Church was demolished in 1846.

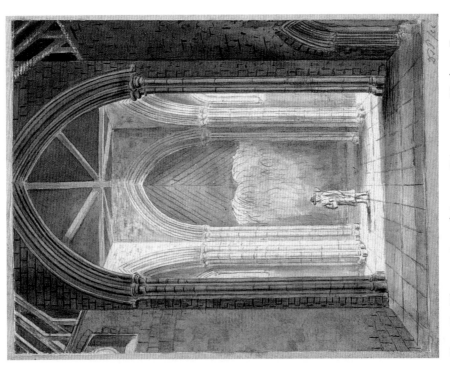

Plate 11 The remains of Latton Priory, near Harlow, Essex, sketched by David Thomas Powell in about 1795.

Plate 13   Hatchments of the Wroth family of Loughton drawn by David Thomas Powell. Originally in St Nicholas's Church, Loughton.

Plate 14   Hatchments of the Wroth family of Loughton drawn by David Thomas Powell. Originally in St Nicholas's Church, Loughton.

Plate 15 Loughton Hall sketched by David Thomas Powell in 1790. The Hall was destroyed by fire in 1836.

Plate 16 Greensted Church, near Ongar, Essex, sketched by David Thomas Powell in about 1800.

Plate 17   St Nicholas's Chapel, Coggeshall, Essex, sketched by David Thomas Powell in about 1800.

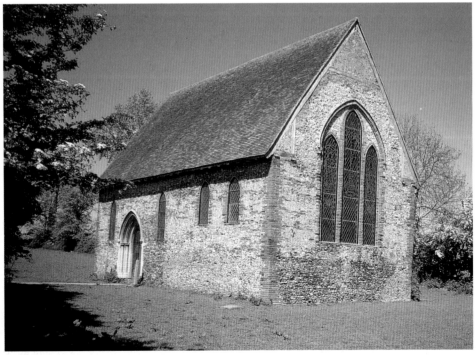

Plate 18   St Nicholas's Chapel, Coggeshall, Essex, in 2002.

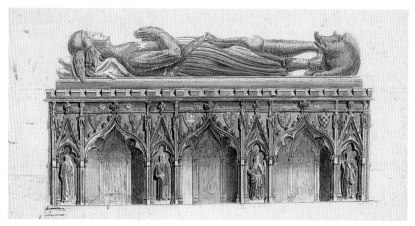

Plate 19 Monument to the 5th Earl of Oxford sketched by David Thomas Powell at the time that it was in Earls Colne Parish Church, Essex.

Plate 20 Monument to the 11th Earl of Oxford and his Countess sketched by David Thomas Powell at the time that it was in Earls Colne Parish Church, Essex.

Plate 21 St Mary's Church, Little Dunmow, Essex, formerly the Lady Chapel of Dunmow Priory, sketched by David Thomas Powell in 1803.

Plate 22 Transitional-Norman arches in St Mary's Church, Little Dunmow, in 2002.

Plate 23   St Osyth's Priory, Essex, sketched by David Thomas Powell in 1816.

Plate 24   St Osyth's Priory, Essex, sketched by David Thomas Powell in 1816.

Plate 25   Hedingham Castle, Essex, sketched by David Thomas Powell in 1806.

Plate 26   Interior (Banqueting Hall) of Hedingham Castle in 2002.

Plate 27   St Luke's Hospital, Old Street, London, in 1831.

Plate 28   East Horndon Church, Essex, where Harry Powell was Rector from 1795–1831.

Plate 29   North Door of East Horndon Church, Essex.

Buckhurst Hill

Drawn by R C Caswall 1872

Plate 30 Luctons House, Buckhurst Hill, Essex. The home of Nathanael Powell from 1855–1906. Painted by R C Caswall in 1872. (Waltham Forest Archives)

Parts of Chingford Hall survived until 20–30 years ago, but the old church has survived. In 1844 a new church was built at Chingford Green, and the dedication of St Peter & St Paul was transferred to that church, the older church reverting to its original dedication. After 1844 All Saints was used only for occasional services and it gradually became a picturesque ruin. However, a thorough restoration was completed in 1930, thanks to a substantial gift from Miss Louisa Heathcote. Plate 10 shows the church sketched by David Thomas Powell.

East Ham

Powell visited East Ham Church, which he found very interesting. However, he first describes, in an attractive piece of travel writing, his journey to East Ham:

A new road paved in the middle leads in a straight line to the newly made East India Docks. On the right just by the road I observed Limehouse Church a very large magnificent building with a tower all of Portland stone and on the left over the fields the square tower of Stepney. At the end of the wall of the India Docks the River Lea almost at its confluence with the Thames runs north and south parting the counties [Middlesex and Essex] over which a bridge principally of iron has just been built and had only been opened a day or two [before] I passed it over – it consists of three circular arches and two highly pointed gothic of iron on iron pillars and is a curious piece of mechanism.

By means of this bridge I saved nearly two miles to the object of my journey, East Ham, for from it a road just passable leads in a direct straight line east and west through this marsh and the view all round is filled with rich fertile fields, and on the right the river and Shooters Hill with the vast variety of buildings and shipping and at a mile from this bridge I passed a Public House at Plaistow bearing the sign of the [Stratford] Abbey arms well painted and it would seem if it were got from some authority. On proceeding about two miles along the new road I turned to the right over several fields till I came to the small village of East Ham and then the road leading to Blackwall led me to the church which stands quite alone and in a situation among fertile meadows sequestered and beautifully commanding a fine view on the south to the river and the Kentish hills just over Woolwich and due west an extensive prospect over a great tract of level ground to London.

Powell describes the church as 'a more interesting church or more countryfied I have scarcely met in the most distant parts of the Kingdom than this and considering all things in a very perfect and pristine state'. There are two sketches of the church: an exterior view (Plate 6) and part of the Westmorland monument about which he has much to say. Powell refers to the entry in Lysons' *Environs of London* for East Ham Church and says that it is wrong in referring to two chancels and that in describing the Arms of the Earl of Westmorland he made errors and omissions. Although today situated in an urban area, this important Norman church has the distinction of having one of the largest churchyards in England. It is over nine acres and, although closed for burials, it is now also a nature reserve supervised by the London Borough of Newham

Latton

The old priory at Latton, which Powell notes is about 21 miles from Whitechapel, is visited on another journey:

Situated on a small eminence at some distance from the road from Epping to Harlow on the left in a very beautiful sequestered situation surrounded within woods. A part of the church remains converted into a barn, it is in the form of a cross at the intersection of which are four grand arches on clustered cylinders which doubtlessly once supported the tower, though the east part is pulled down and a wooden barn erected on its site, it is plain how far it extended that way. The two crosses or transepts are entire, each terminated with a large window deprived of tracery and mountings, the arch of the north one and the pediment above is destroyed, but only a few feet westward from the main arches remains the nave, nor is it easy to say how far it extended. On the north side of the nave evidently was the cloister from the north circular window high up in the wall – but there is no remnant of it – at all the angles were buttresses – the nave, crosses and chancel are about eighteen feet in breadth – and from the style of the whole I judge it was erected towards the latter part of the reign of King Henry III, the four centre arches have much the air of the four centre ones of Westminster Abbey on a smaller scale. The whole was moated, great part of which remains.

Powell quotes the Essex historian, Rev Philip Morant, who in 1768 had published his *History and Antiquities of the County of Essex,* a copy of which Powell had in his library. Four watercolour sketches are included, together with a plan of the likely layout of the priory. The remains of the priory exist to this day. (Plate 11.)

Loughton

In making his journey to Latton Priory, Powell would have travelled through Epping Forest passing close to, if not through, the village of Loughton, where as we have seen other members of the Powell family lived. He is impressed by the area:

This church [St Nicholas] is situated in a beautiful and retired country about a mile and a half from the Epping road on a high ground commanding at some distance off a vast prospect over Essex into Kent, and I should think Sussex [more likely Surrey]. The village which consists of detached farms and cottages skirting on the Forest and spread over the extensive parish though so near town was in my remembrance as rural and the people of as pristine manners as in most remote parts of England.

   The church is a small structure and consists of a nave divided from a north side aisle by some arches, a chancel with a chapel or chantry off it, as I suppose, as it has a wood gothic screen dividing it from the north aisle. At the west end is a pretty wood tower with a shingled octagon from a square pyramid. On the south side the nave is entered by an ancient gabled porch the pediment adorned with gothic trefoils as usual in ancient porches and a niche once containing a figure. The East window of the chancel and chapel are the only windows worth observation: they are of the later gothic of three compartments with perpendicular mountings subdivided in the arch in six gothic compartments as usual. I did not observe any signs of remote antiquity about the building.

In the chapel on the north side of the chancel, which now belongs to Miss Whitacre [*sic*] the Lady of the Manor, against the walls are several Hatchments of the eminent family of Wroth which are here drawn. Their burial place is here but there is no memorial or inscription whatsoever to them, not even the name except these Hatchments, some of which, decayed by age, have lately been taken down. The vault is only distinguished by an iron railing enclosing a small space on the north side. On the altar step is a stone inlaid with a brass effigy of a man in armour, which I have not yet examined, but Morant[5] says 'John Stonard, gent. who died 19 June 1541, is buried in the north aisle of the chancel of this church, with his wives, Joane and Catherine. George Stonard presented to this rectory in 1554, jointly with Edward Stacy. And the said George dying 25 of November 1558, was buried in the same aisle, with his wife Mary. At the man's feet, were the effigies of six daughters. Francis Stonard Esq. One of the sons, died 13 of September 1604.'

In ye nave an old brass or two which I had not time to examine.

1713 – from the parish registers – At the church a workman for one day and 2 bushels of lime – 3d, a gallon of Tent [red sacramental wine] – 11s.

There are two watercolour sketches of St Nicholas's Church, one of which is dated 1790. (Plate 12.)

Extensive notes are included by Powell on the history of the Wroth family together with three watercolour drawings of Wroth hatchments. (Plates 13 and 14.)

In the next folio Powell goes on to describe the manor house:

Loughton Hall [Plate 15], the manor house stands a small distance north west of the church: it is a large building of brick edged with stone and has several pillars of the Grecian order attached to the front. I have heard that Inigo Jones built it. There is an extensive forecourt with brick walls, the entrance to which is by a large handsome open iron gate having above it the cypher doubled of John Whitaker and the crest of Wroth. By the decease of Miss Whitaker [in] 1825 this Hall, Manor etc went to Anthony Hamilton Esq of Woodford [Powell was incorrect here, the Manor was sold to John Maitland of Woodford Hall]. The Hall and a library of books and MSS said to be worth £20,000 was consumed by the fire in Jan 1837 [the fire was actually in December 1836]. Miss Whitaker occasionally resided at Loughton Hall and kept it exactly in the state it was in Captain Wroth's time, but she principally lived in Kensington where she was a very formal etequette [*sic*] lady of the old school or court and reconn'd very rich living in a good style. She had been sought in marriage when young by some even of rank and title, but ever avoided it. She died in Kensington and was here interred in 1825.

Powell's notes and sketches of St Nicholas's Church and Loughton Hall are an invaluable record as the church was demolished in 1845, following a decision to build a new church a mile to the west, where the main population of the village had developed by the middle of the nineteenth century. The fire at Loughton Hall in 1836 effectively destroyed the building which was subsequently demolished and a new hall built, albeit not until forty years later. The churchyard at St Nicholas's remains as a record of the well known families of Loughton throughout the seventeenth and eighteenth centuries.[6] A small memorial chapel was built in 1876, slightly to the east of the old church.

Coggeshall

One of David Thomas Powell's longer journeys into Essex was to Coggeshall, which he noted is 43 miles from Whitechapel Church. During his visit he was fortunate to meet the owner of the remaining abbey buildings, who was obviously delighted to show him around and to explain their history:

At Coggeshall Magna these things I observed, ascending a hill to the highest part of the town a large church [St Peter-ad-Vincula] with a tower and fine windows of the time Edward IV but all the painted glass has gone: the east end of the chancel more modern with the buttress at corners so elegant that I drew and measured them. [The nave and tower were severely damaged in the Second World War in the 1940s.]

Descending, and at about three quarters of a mile from the church in a low ground of a very damp or swampy appearance and with streams of water running through it, is situated the small remains of a once great Cistercian abbey now converted into a farm occupied by a Quaker who was very obliging in this research, adjoining whose dwelling house (which is part of the abbey offices) is a barn built of red brick with four fine small lancet windows of brick also, the first I had ever seen of that material and at first sight I took them to be modern but on examination I soon found that they were coeval with the original building of the monastery. On going into the house the Quaker showed me a vaulted room entirely built of brick with groins also of brick which are for the most part covered with a compos like mortar and whitewash painted with red lines of masonry but where that has fallen off the bricks are seen most nicely put together in so much that, however well they may have managed their compos it seems a pity to have covered them. I was shown a doorway or two, the mouldings of the gothic arch particularly remarkable for the curious way in which the bricks are cut to form them. Came to the remains of a small beautiful window, the arch of deep mouldings, the pillars with capitals resembling those of Netely Abbey, this at first appears to me to be made of stone but I found it was a composition resembling it. The Quaker informed me that stone was not to be found about here but excellent brick earth.

This whole building of brick compos is a curious circumstance which I have not met with before and admirable is the invention of the monks to suit all situations yet here they seem not to have approved of the appearance of brick though they had the art of laying them together with such superlative niceness and strength for it appears from the remains that all the walls as well as the windows were covered with the compos to give them the appearance of stone. I observed that many of the walls have a very rough appearance being composed of flint rubble and long red tyles very like Roman tyles put together with very strong mortar and then covered with compos which doubtless was marked with lines of masonry, though in these exposed walls from lapse of so many ages there is but small remains of it.

The Quaker informed me that the conventual church stood in a field adjoining his house and was square according to his account of the foundations which appear in very dry weather. He had at different times seen small ornamental tyles.

From hence ascending a little I came to a small original chapel of St Nicholas, (as it would seem), now turned into a barn which is very perfect and of which I took a view within, the splays and mountings of the east window is painted on the stucco with red arrabesque flowers in a free masterly manner, the east and west ends of this building have three long narrows lancet windows within a pointed arch, they are, however, filled up. The two sides have small lancet windows in them though one side has been partly broke away to make a large barn door.

The abbey was never moated, though partly surrounded with water. The bridge is original, built of bricks and very strong.

During his visit Powell made water colour sketches of the remains of the abbey and St Nicholas's Chapel. The particular importance of Coggeshall Abbey lies in the fact that brick was used as a primary building material at all periods of its history. There is ample evidence at Coggeshall to show that bricks of excellent quality were being made in England by the middle of the twelfth century. Coggeshall Abbey was founded in 1140 by King Stephen. It survived until February 1538 when the abbey and all its estates were surrendered to the Crown. Within three years the Church was 'clene prostrate' and demolition of the cloister and other buildings followed by 1581, when the Crown lease was held by the Paycocke family. One of the original buildings which remains is the Guest House. After the Dissolution a house was built into the abbey premises.

As we have seen, Powell visited the gatehouse chapel of St Nicholas, some one hundred yards west of the abbey church, and which for more than 300 years after the Dissolution was used as a barn. In 1860 it was acquired by the then vicar of Coggeshall and restoration commenced. However, it was not until 1890 that this was completed. The lancet windows were opened up and the East Window now has attractive stained glass. The thatch roof of Powell's sketch has been replaced by tiles and the porch removed. The chapel is thought to have been built in c 1220 and is once again used for Divine Service (Plates 17 and 18).[7]

Navestock and Greensted

Two short notes on the churches at Navestock and Greensted are worthy of quotation:

Navestock: In a very beautiful country the church is situated at a small distance from the road near to Lord Waldegrave's park. Eastward in the chancel it has some good windows of the Marlow kind with scraps of painted glass, preserved in one a border of lyons of England. The porch into the nave of oak wood, like Loughton a gable finely ornamented with little gothic arches in the spandrils. Set in gothic works are two shields of the arms, much defaced by time, of Fitzwalter but its overall appearance is lost by a modern white painting instead of its venerable oak covered with moss.

The timber south porch was destroyed by a landmine in 1940, as was the stained glass. Restoration was completed in 1954 and the church, which dates from the eleventh or twelfth century, remains one of the most attractive in Essex.

Greensted near Chipping Ongar: This church is said to be of a very remote antiquity and has been the subject of plans and sections in a copper plate published . . . [no date is given]. The nave walls are built of the trunks of trees split or sawn asunder and fixed in the ground. In the east window of the chancel is this wheatsheaf in painted glass, it may have some reference to some of the possessors of the manor. For my part I have doubts as to the very remote antiquity of the church which they talk so much about here. [Plate 16.]

The debate about the age of Greensted church has continued over the 200 years since Powell made his observations. It was originally thought to have been constructed in 850, but recent tree-ring dating has suggested a date around the Conquest, in the late eleventh century.

Earls Colne

A topographical history of Essex would be incomplete without a reference to the Earls of Oxford and the de Vere family. Earls Colne is one of four neighbouring villages in the Colne Valley to which the river has given its name. They are Colne Engaine, Earls Colne, Wakes Colne and White Colne. In addition to their castle at Hedingham, the Earls of Oxford had a palace at Colne. Thus it was the Colne village in which they lived that became known as Earls Colne. Powell visited the village and learned much about its history:

The once great monastery here is so totally destroyed that not only one stone remains not on the other but there is not a stone of the whole fabric to be found on the site. It stood in a low ground at some distance from the church and town watered by the river Colne, a small stream running into the German Ocean [North Sea]. A large red brick house occupies a part of the monastic site inhabited and belonging to the Rev Mr Carwardine to whom it descended as heir at law to the Harlakendens, one of whom was steward to the de Vere family and enriched himself at the expense of his lord, so said Mr Carwardine. Gardens, lawns etc fill up the remaining space of the abbey site, about twelve acres.

It is to the parish church therefore that we are obliged to go for any remains of antiquity in this place, where fortunately three monuments of the most illustrious family of the founder of the priory are preserved having been removed from the priory hither, but what is become of the rest even those described by Daniel King to have been remaining in his time I could not discover. Most likely they have been used for some base purpose of the farm or household convenience.

The church, dedicated to St Andrew, is nothing more than an ordinary parish church consisting of a handsome tower at the west end built by and adorned at the top with the Gartered arms and quartered badges of John de Vere, Earl of Oxford in the time of Henry VIII, and dated 1538, a nave and chancel adorned with smaller windows of much tracery of about the time of Edward I. A side aisle or chantry off the nave contains nothing remarkable, the east window and the two side ones deprived of their original tracery and mountings.

Powell goes on to describe the three monuments to the Earls of Oxford, the first of which is to Robert de Vere, the fifth Earl of Oxford:

Against the north wall of the chancel stands a superb altar monument, deprived of its surbase, the side and two ends of which are adorned with niches and small statues and coats of arms, the cornice finished with embattlements, on it lays a noble figure cross legged of an Earl of Oxford, his head supported by two angels, at his feet a blue boar, he is in mail from head to foot with a loose surcoat of his arms with sword and military bret round his brows and head a circle adorned with studded work by way of coronets, his shield gone, his hands have been joined in prayer but the whole statue and monument shamefully, yet by no means fatally destroyed. The shield which was on his left arm torn away, but the strap that attached it remains. The four panels of which three are seen contain sixteen shields: 6 north and south, 2 head or west, 2 feet or south. The whole shows great remains of painting and gilding.

Gough in his sepulchural monuments gives this as the monument of Robert de Vere, Earl of Oxford, who died twenty-fourth [year] of Edward I's [reign] and describes these arms taken from a MS which accompanying Daniel King's draft made in 1653 now in Mr Walpole's collection by whose favour (he says) this is exhibited. He gives a view of this fine tomb, vile in the extreme, done by a person of name of Tyson. The outline copied into Gough's work from Daniel King's draft is not to say badly done but very much incorrect in so much that I could have done it better from recollection. The monument itself is represented strangely distorted and difficult to be understood. The saints are represented in a strange way and no difference made between those that are painted in the backs of the broad niches, and those which are in alto relief in the smaller ones he calls it a through east view. This is a rough sketch of it just to show how the arms were in King's time who has probably given them correct. [Here is inserted Powell's sketch.]

Mr Gough makes the following observation: This monument was moved at the dissolution into the parish church [from the priory] and placed in the middle of the chancel since which it has been again moved and placed against the north wall of the chancel, how superb the altar part of this monument must have been we may plainly see by King's draft since round it there were twenty four painted saints and twelve statues in alto relief in the niches.

Powell continues with his detailed description of the other two effigies in the church at the time of his visit when he also made five watercolour sketches and several pencil drawings of the tombs (Plates 19 and 20). He refers to the three de Vere monuments to the fifth, eighth and eleventh Earls being moved from the priory to the parish church. In 1827 they were returned to the priory at which time Henry Holgate Carwardine had pulled down the old structure on the site and built a new house to the south of the former one. He brought back the three surviving effigies, together with that for Alice Sergeaux, the Countess of the eleventh Earl, and put them in a specially built gallery in his new home. However, in 1935, to the sorrow of all Colne people, they were moved to St Stephens Chapel, Bures, in Suffolk.[8]

In 1862–64 a 'thorough restoration' of the parish church took place in which a new north aisle, north chapel and south chapel were built. This necessitated reconstructing the chancel and at the same time the south porch was rebuilt.[9]

Dunmow Priory

Powell includes a short note on a visit to Little Dunmow and includes some very attractive sketches (see Plate 21):

Founded in AD 1104 by Juga Baynard, sister of Ralph Baynard. This priory consisted of a Prior and 10 or 11 Canons Regular of the order of Saint Augustine and at its suppression valued at from £150–173, which was granted to Robert Radcliffe, Earl of Sussex, since, it has passed through various hands. The church was consecrated by Maurice, Bishop of London; Saer de Quincy, Earl of Winchester, Roger de Cantabrigg were benefactors. All the oblations in the chapel in this parish belonging to the Lord Fitzwalter's house were given to this Priory.

The monastery which is now entirely razed was pleasantly situated on a rising ground, foundations of the old building are visible. The present manor house stands where the offices of the Priory were.

All that remains today is the Lady (south) chapel, which is now the parish church. The church underwent a major renovation and re-ordering during the 1870s to the designs of the well known church architect Fred Chancellor. His work included a new East Window, the somewhat incongruous Bell Tower (turret), and two additional buttresses on the south wall. However, it is in the interior that the church's glory is seen. The arches forming the arcade on the north side are from the twelfth century and display some of the richest Norman-Transitional carving in Essex (Plate 22). The west wall is thirteenth century. The south wall has four magnificent fourteenth century windows with differing designs of stone tracery (the glass is recent). The church is now partly surrounded by modern housing.

Pedigrees of Essex families

In addition to the volume on Essex churches and other buildings, Powell produced a portfolio of the pedigrees and arms of Essex families. This consists of heraldic drawings in colour, pedigree charts and text of some of the ancient families of the county, including the Bourchiers, Tyrells, 'Walgraves' (Waldegraves) and Darcys. There are 54 folios.[10]

Other counties

The surviving volumes for the other counties follow a similar format to the Essex portfolio. In passing we may note that Powell had little to say about the 'other' Loughton in Buckinghamshire:

This church contains little of interest. The tower is prop'd with a buttress against its west door and window. There are some good windows about the building. Arches of nave H. III.

There is no sketch of the church. Historians with an interest in Buckinghamshire and Bedfordshire (the portfolios are combined into one volume) will, however, find much to study in the extensive number of folios.[11]

Legacy

The principal legacy which remains of David Thomas Powell's work is undoubtedly his drawings and sketches, mostly in colour, of churches and manor houses, made 200 years ago. His knowledge of ecclesiastical architecture is demonstrated in his accompanying text. If the details of the history of a particular village appear on occasion to be slight, he makes no apology for this and instead quotes better qualified sources such as, in the case of Essex, Philip Morant. Where Powell gives a description of his journey to a particular village or church, his writing adds to the delight of his ultimate objective. Some of the buildings that Powell drew no longer exist and others have been substantially altered. His work will remain as an illustrated topographical survey of England and Wales just before Victorian enthusiasm for restoration came to destroy much that was old in our churches and other buildings.

REFERENCES

1. British Library Add MS 22505.
2. British Library Add MSS 17436 and 17438.
3. British Library Add MS 17694.
4. British Library Add MS 17460.
5. Morant, P, *History and Antiquities of County of Essex* (1768).
6. Waller, W C, 'Some Account of the Vanished Church of St Nicholas', EAS Trans 1916.
7. Gardner, J S, 'Coggeshall Abbey and its Early Brickwork', *Journal of the British Archaeological Association* (1955).
8. *Essex Review*, vol LIII, pp 13–22.
9. St Andrews Church, *A Short History and Guide*.
10. British Library Add MS 17461.
11. British Library Add MS 17456.

4

Bench House, Loughton, Essex

Loughton in Essex lies some eleven miles north-east of the City of London and is surrounded on the west and north by Epping Forest. The eastern boundary of the parish is the River Roding. From Saxon times until the middle of the nineteenth century, Loughton was very much a forest village with, in 1851, a population of 1,237. The coming of the railway in 1856 and the expansion of the east London suburbs led to the growth of the village in the second half of the nineteenth century and, by the middle of the twentieth, it had become a commuter town although preserving its forest surroundings thanks to the Epping Forest Act of 1878.

In 1861 Coller, a Victorian historian, described it as:

A very picturesque village, and ground of remarkably undulating character. The views and scenery in this village are equal to almost anything of the kind in this part of England with views extending to the Thames and Kentish Hills in one direction and to Hampstead and Highgate in another.[1]

Bench House, Loughton, Essex, in 1784

Baden Powell (1731–1802)

Perhaps this is why, in 1772, Baden Powell, the second eldest surviving son of David and Susannah Powell, decided to come to live in Loughton. Baden had not married but, as we have seen, worked in the family business with his younger brother James. He purchased the Bench House estate which lay at the southern end of Loughton to the east of the road from London. William Waller described the estate in his history of Loughton[2]:

Abutting on North's Farm, with a frontage extending thence, with one small exception [the Bull's Head and six adjacent cottages] to beyond the Bull's Head, is the estate which down to 1854 belonged to the Powell family. It was made up of several holdings of various sizes, no longer to be certainly identified, although a few ancient names have survived. To set out the vicissitudes of ownership in detail would be tedious, and it will be most convenient to indicate groups in which the fields and houses appear first in the Rolls.

In 1619 William Dawges was admitted to Bench House and Burton Field, five acres, the quit rent being 2d. He made them over in 1638 to William Warren, whose descendant, nearly a hundred years after, sold them to John Hart, who about the same time acquired other [nearby] land.

In 1676 Richard Stock died owning or occupying seventy acres of land in Loughton, much of it near Bench House. This included the twenty three acres of Great Mead and eleven acres of Stanleyes. [Waller lists all the fields.] In 1642 William and Margaret Rutland were possessed of a messuage, garden and eighteen acres in Loughton Street, of which three closes, out of five were said in 1698 to be near Common Lane, which led from Loughton Street east to Baker's Hill. In 1702 the property was acquired by John Bale, whose son, Sackville, succeeded him.

From 1593 a house called Hills and five acres of land remained in the possession of the Dawges family until, in 1692, it passed to John Low, who made it over to his son in 1727.

In 1675 Richard Stock possessed and parted with a 2½ acre close of meadow, Cowle [Cold] Bakers, abutting on the highway [Loughton Street] on the north west and on the land of J Warren on the south east. This passed in 1704 to a son of the owner of Hills.

The ultimate consolidation of all these various properties into one began in 1772 when Mr Baden Powell acquired Bench House and Great Mead. In 1783 he bought Cole[Cold]bakers and Hills. [A sketch of Bench House in 1784 is shown on page 34.] The house referred to as Hills was probably the previous name of what became known as Willow Cottage [now replaced by a block of flats].

Baden Powell also purchased land in the nearby parish of Theydon Bois. A house, garden and meadows, in total over 14 acres, was acquired on the southern side of Loughton Lane near its junction with The Green. Another 18 acres of farmland was purchased on either side of Coopersale Lane.

Little, if anything, is known of Baden's life during the 30 years that he spent at Loughton. The return in 1780 for the male servants' tax showed that he had one servant. However, it is reasonable to assume that he received visits from his numerous nephews and nieces who lived at Homerton and Clapton and, in the case of David Thomas Powell, who rode

David Powell (1764–1832)

over from Tottenham. There is, however, one undated letter in verse form which, if its provenance is valid, indicates that Baden's hospitality was appreciated. The letter is addressed to Mr B Powell, Crown Buildings, Broad Street:

> Within this pleasing rural lot
> On downy head has been my lot
> To sleep. I heard with sudden moan
> The tempest beat against the door.
> Sunk in the downy arms of sleep
> Methought I heard a Traveller weep
> Who wandering in a dreamy dell
> Made trackless by the snow which fell
> Met no kind voice or cheering light
> To guide his fainting steps aright.
> He thy good Genius brought thee where
> Baden Powell spreads his hospitable fare
> His friendly voice had heard thy soul
> His generous hand had filled the bowl.
> Made thee forget thy sorrow o'er
> And bless thy stars which led
> Thee to his door.[3]

Baden Powell died on 31 August 1802 at his brother's house at Clapton, in his seventy-second year. He had both inherited and amassed himself considerable wealth in both his personal estate, which was valued at £95,000, and his real estate. As he had no children of his own, his estate was left to his brother James and his 17 nephews and nieces, with some small legacies to other related friends.

His brother James received the residue of the personal estate which was estimated at £27,000, together with the estate at Wattisfield in Suffolk. The estates at Walsham-le-Willows and at Theydon Bois were left to his nephew, John Clark Powell. The main estate, at Loughton, was left to his nephew, David Powell.

Baden was buried in the family vault in the churchyard at St John's, Hackney.

David Powell (1764–1832)

Baden's nephew, David, the second eldest son of David and Laetitia Powell, was born in Little St Helens, London, in November 1764. He joined the family business in the City and in December 1798 married Mary Townsend. Soon after their marriage they must have moved to Walthamstow, a few miles into Essex over the River Lea, as their first child, Harry Townsend Powell, was baptised at St Mary's Church in Walthamstow early in 1800. However, their stay in Walthamstow was short as, following the death of his

Mary Powell (1775–1809)

Grizell Powell (1781–1852)

uncle, Baden, in 1802, David moved to Bench House at Loughton. Shortly after his arrival at Bench House, David expanded the estate by the purchase of further adjoining land. The total estate then extended to more than 120 acres. Appendix D gives a plan of the estate based on the Ordnance Survey edition of 1871, and the sale of the estate in 1899.

David and Mary Powell had six children, two sons and four daughters. Three of the daughters were to be married in St Nicholas Church, Loughton. David, the younger of the two sons, became a Director of the Bank of England and in due course his son, also David, was to become Deputy Governor of the Bank of England. Mary Powell died at Loughton in March 1809 and lies buried in the churchyard of St Nicholas.

In August 1810 David married Grizell Hoare, the youngest daughter of Samuel Hoare, the banker, and she came to live at Loughton. Seven children were to be born at Loughton of this second marriage; four daughters and three sons. They were all baptised in St Nicholas Church.

On Tuesday, 15 May 1832, David Powell was walking in the grounds of his estate at Loughton, when he was caught in a thunderstorm. *The Times* newspaper on the following Monday, 21 May, included the following report:

A most melancholy and fatal instance of the danger of seeking shelter under a tree during a thunderstorm occurred on Tuesday last, at Loughton, in this county, in the death of David Powell Esq of that place. During the violent storm which came on in the afternoon of that day, the deceased, who had been walking in his grounds, was observed to go under a high elm, and place himself close against the body of the tree. Within a minute succeeded a most vivid flash of lightning, followed, or it might rather be said accompanied, by a tremendous burst of thunder, and the electric fluid striking the tree under which Mr Powell had taken refuge, reached him in its descent, and his instantaneous death was the consequence. Some labourers in his employ, who happened to be near the spot, on going up found their master a lifeless corpse. It appeared that the fatal fluid had gone completely down the body, from the head to the feet of the deceased. His right side, from his face downwards was much discoloured; his shirt, particularly at the neck, as well as other parts of his clothes, was very much scorched, and his boots were literally shivered into small fragments. His watch and eyeglass were uninjured. The deceased, who was a magistrate of this county, and most deservedly esteemed and respected, has left a disconsolate widow and thirteen children to lament their irreparable loss. Mrs Powell and several of her daughters had that morning gone to London, and little anticipating the melancholy and overwhelming spectacle which awaited them on their return. The regret evinced by all classes on this melancholy event served to show the estimation in which Mr Powell was held in his circle and neighbourhood.

The report in *The Times* was in fact a reprint of the report that had appeared in the previous Saturday's edition of the *Essex Standard*, published at Colchester. Obituaries appeared in other local newspapers. David Powell had been a Deputy Lieutenant for Essex and was widely known throughout the county. He was buried in the churchyard at St Nicholas, alongside his first wife.

Grizell Powell continued to live at Bench House with her large family for the next 20 years. When the new parish church of St John's, Loughton was built in 1845, Grizell made a very substantial donation towards the cost and also gave the Communion Table. She died in February 1852, after which the estate was put up for sale. A slight confusion arises here as at some time in the first half of the nineteenth century a new house had been built on the site. This has on occasion been described on maps as Beech House, but should not be confused with the nearby Beech House Farm, which formed part of the estate. Bench House was to further change its name by about 1890 to Newnham House.

The notice for the sale of the house in May 1852 gave the following description:

EXCELLENT AND SUBSTANTIAL RESIDENCE,
BEAUTIFULLY SITUATE IN THE FOREST AT LOUGHTON,
NEAR WOODFORD WITH ABOUT 120 ACRES OF LAND

Messrs Hoggart, Norton and Trist have received instruction from the Trustees of the late David Powell Esq to offer for sale at the Mart, on Friday, May 21 at 12 noon, a substantially built family residence beautifully situate on the Forest at Loughton, near Woodford, containing nine bedrooms including servants rooms, two dressing rooms, water closets, entrance hall, dining room, drawing room, library and study, well arranged servants offices and good cellars. Detached stabling for nine horses, coach houses, loft and man's room, lawn, pleasure grounds, productive gardens, orchards and meadow land; at a short distance is a range of farm buildings, three cottages and a small shop and dwelling house, with offices and a garden, also a compact farm, with farm house, barns and every requisite farm building, with several enclosures of useful arable and meadow land, with valuable forest rights.

The whole estate containing about 120 acres. The farm and about 100 acres are in the occupation of Mr Chilton, at a rental of £150 per annum. The cottages are let, and of the estimated value of £15 per annum, and the shop and dwelling house is let to Mr Hill at a rental of £16 per annum, leaving the house offices, garden etc and about 14 acres of meadowland in hand. The estate is copyhold of the manor of Loughton.

May be viewed and particulars had at The Castle, Woodford; Eagle, Snaresbrook of Messrs Pemberton and Crawley, 20 Whitehall Place at the Mart; and of Messrs Hoggart, Norton and Trist, 62 Old Broad Street, Royal Exchange.

The contents of the main house were sold at a separate sale on the premises a month later. The whole estate was sold to John Low. In 1899 the estate was again sold and in 1919 the house, which since about 1890 had been called Newnham House, together with eight acres, was separately sold again. In 1954-5 most of the garden of Newnham House, was sold and developed to form 1-27 Spring Grove and Newnham Close. The house, was demolished in about 1963 to be replaced by a block of flats.

In 1909 the remaining freehold estate of 93 acres, which was made up of Beech House Farm, the old Bulls Head Inn (by then converted into a cottage), Willow Cottage, and a modern villa called Overmist in a recently made road cut through the estate, called Spring Grove, was sold by the executors of Andrew Pears to Messrs Gould. Much of the arable land was developed with new roads and houses to form the Beech Hill Park Estate. (It is generally now known as the Spring Grove estate.)

The particulars of the old farmhouse in the sale described it as:

A very picturesque old fashioned residence (dated 1648) containing, on the ground floor a square hall, good drawing and dining rooms, large kitchen and offices. On the upper floor, six bedrooms, one panelled with carved oak, bathroom and WC. In the basement a cellar.

The house had on its front a brick panel with the inscription:

```
            R
   W              M
         1648
           IR
   Age            4
```

The inscription refers to William Rutland and his wife Margaret. The latter survived her husband, and by a will dated 8 September 1688 bequeathed the property (then in the occupation of John Low, butcher) to her grandson, William Hart, son of her daughter Sarah.[4]

The estate at Theydon Bois, two miles north-east of Loughton, which Baden Powell had left to his nephew, John Clark Powell, descended to John Clark Powell's nephew, John Cotton Powell, on the former's death in 1847. The Tithe Award of 1849 for Theydon Bois shows John Cotton Powell as the owner-occupier of a house on the corner of Loughton Lane and The Green. He was also the owner, but not occupier, of the land in Coopersale Lane. However, by 1891 he was living at East Grinstead, although he may have still owned the estate for a little longer.

The Powells' links with Essex continued throughout the nineteenth century as Agnes, the daughter of David and Grizell Powell, married her cousin Nathanael Powell and they lived first at Walthamstow and then, in 1855, moved to Buckhurst Hill where they were to remain for the rest of their lives, and bring up 12 of their 13 children (Robert had died in infancy in Walthamstow.) Nathanael Powell's life at Luctons, Buckhurst Hill, is described in Chapter 7.

REFERENCES

1. Coller, D W, *The People's History of Essex* (1861), p 486.
2. Waller, W C, *Loughton in Essex* (1900), pp 111–112.
3. Vestry House Museum, Powell Scrapbooks, vol 4, f 53.
4. Thompson, P, *Notebooks on Loughton,* vol 1, City of London Guildhall Library.

5

St Luke's Hospital

On 13 June 1750, six gentlemen of the City of London met at the King's Arms Tavern in Exchange Alley to discuss the establishment of a new hospital for poor lunatics. Two of the six, James Sperling and Thomas Light, were described as Merchants of Mincing Lane.

London already had Bethlem Hospital:

A noble and extensive charity from which the public have much benefit as can be reasonably expected; but it is well known that this hospital is incapable of receiving and maintaining the great number of melancholy objects of this sort who apply for relief.[1]

The law had made no particular provision for lunatics and many were to be found in the parish workhouse, living alongside other old and infirm inmates. People with other illnesses were admitted without delay to hospital but persons with mental illness only had Bethlem in London. The six City gentlemen were of the opinion that a charity established for the purpose of building such a new hospital would meet with encouragement from the public. It was agreed to open a subscription list and as soon as £1,000 had been promised there should be a meeting to elect a president, treasurer and secretary. A further meeting in June was told that six apothecaries of the City were willing to supply the proposed hospital with drugs and medicines free of charge for the next three years.

It was proposed that each subscriber who gave 20 guineas and upwards, or paid five guineas in each of four successive years, would become a governor of the hospital for life. The project was well received by the public and sufficient donations were promised to enable the promoters to proceed with finding a site. Three trustees, a committee of 21 governors and a secretary were appointed and in October 1750 the committee reported that they had inspected a site known as the Foundry in Windmill Hill, Upper Moorfields, of which the lease, held from the City of London, was about to expire. Mr George Dance, the City Surveyor, was in sympathy with the project and agreed to provide his services without fee.

Windmill Hill, Upper Moorfields

The Foundry was a large building where formerly cannon had been cast but in 1716 there had been a violent explosion in which several people were killed and many injured. The Foundry ceased operations and fell into disuse. Subsequently it was leased to John Wesley as a place for preaching and for many years it was the centre of his operations and the place where the first Methodist Book-Room was opened. The site is commemorated today by a plaque on the wall of a nearby building towards the southern end of Tabernacle Street, near Worship Street. In November 1750 the Court of Common Council agreed to let the Foundry and some small houses adjoining it to the committee on a 32-year lease. Mr Wesley was allowed to continue his use of the premises until the detailed plans for the alterations to the building had been approved. At the beginning of 1751, carpenters, bricklayers and other tradesmen began converting the building into a hospital, which in June 1751 was given the name St Luke's. It was situated in St Luke's parish and in any case this was an appropriate name for a hospital as St Luke had been a medical man. In July 1751 a few patients were admitted and by January 1752 the committee reported that the hospital was equipped for 26 patients and three resident servants.

While the hospital was being built, a sub-committee had drawn up rules and regulations for its governance. These remain as an excellent example today for any charity. The General Court was to meet twice a year, in February and August, and at the February meeting were to elect a president, four vice-presidents, a treasurer, a general committee, physician, surgeon, apothecary and secretary for the ensuing year. The general committee was to meet each month and should consist of the president, vice-presidents and treasurer, together with 24 other governors. A house committee was also established after the hospital opened and this was required to meet every Friday.

By February 1753 the number of patients had risen to 57 and in 1754 it was decided to readmit incurable patients. The surviving hospital records do not show when the Powell family were first elected as governors of St Luke's but the minutes of the general committee meeting for March 1783 show David Powell (1725–1810) as a member.[2]

By this time the hospital accommodated on average 80 curable and 30 incurable patients but the governors were keen to help more people. They had been left £30,000 in the will of Sir Thomas Clarke, Master of the Rolls, and other donations had put the hospital in a very secure financial position. The governors sought to negotiate with the Corporation of London for a long lease or an outright purchase of the lease together with an extension to the site in Windmill Hill, but without success. However, as early as 1776 the general committee reported that the governors of St Bartholomew's Hospital were prepared to grant a lease for about three acres of ground north of Old Street Road.

John Clark Powell (1763–1847)

Old Street Road

In 1777 an agreement was signed but it was not until 1782 that a plan was approved for the new hospital at an estimated cost of £17,300. The first stone of the new building was laid on 30 July 1782 and work on the building continued until the end of 1786. On 1 January 1787 the patients were transferred from the old to the new hospital. The cost had risen to over £38,000, but the governors now had an excellent building of which they were very proud. (Plate 27.)

Both the committee and the court held meetings in the board room of the new hospital in November 1786. Strictly speaking, therefore, it was no longer necessary for them to meet at various coffee houses and taverns as they had done since the hospital was founded. However, they continued to meet at such places as Batson's Coffee House in Cornhill and the King's Arms Tavern, where no doubt they met other merchants and brokers who became governors of the hospital and contributed much to its success.

The role of the treasurer in the administration of the hospital was emphasised in 1789 when the committee passed a resolution to the effect that the charity owed its institution to William Prowting, Esq, their worthy treasurer, who had been one of the original six City gentlemen who first proposed the founding of the hospital. The treasurer often took the chair at the meetings of the general committee and for the first century of the existence of the hospital effectively performed the role of executive chairman. William Prowting was succeeded as treasurer in 1794 by David Powell. At this time David's son, John Clark Powell, had also been elected as a member of the general committee. By now the assets of the hospital had grown to over £100,000 and the number of patients to over 200. David Powell died in January 1810 and, at meetings of the court and general committee in February, his son, John Clark Powell, was elected treasurer of the hospital.

During the first half of the nineteenth century there were a number of improvements to conditions in the hospital. In 1826 gas was laid into the hospital for the purpose of lighting the galleries, and water closets were made. But heating and ventilation still caused difficulties. Large open fires with smoke and heat pouring up the chimneys were the usual means adopted, and these were built in each of the galleries in 1842. In 1833 it had been recognised that it was important to provide some form of occupational therapy for patients and by 1842 there were reading rooms for both sexes, a piano for dancing, bagatelle tables, cards and draughts.

In 1811 John Clark Powell's brother, Baden, had been elected to the general committee and his younger brother, James, joined the committee in 1820. In 1839 John Clark Powell was elected a vice-president but also continued his role as treasurer. James Powell's son, Arthur, joined the committee following the death of his father in 1840. In addition to those members of the Powell family who were governors and members of the general committee, a list of all the governors of the hospital for 1830 includes David Powell of Loughton and the Rev Harry Powell of East Horndon in Essex.[3]

At the meeting of the general committee in February 1843, John Clark Powell expressed the wish, due to his advanced age, not to be re-elected treasurer. He was now 80 and had served as treasurer for 33 years and had served on the committee for one year short of half a century. The court had recognised his service to the hospital a few years earlier when, in 1839, the general committee met specially at St Luke's, having been requested by the house committee to see the portrait of Mr Powell painted by Mr John Irvine, a patient, who received 45 guineas, subscribed by the gentlemen of the committee and physicians. The fine portrait hangs today in the entrance hall at St Luke's-Woodside Hospital.

John Clark Powell remained a vice-president of St Luke's after his resignation as treasurer, and we find him in the chair at a meeting of the general committee held at the George and Vulture in February 1844. His brother, Baden, died in July 1844 and in May 1847 John Clark Powell died and was buried in the family vault at St John's Church, Hackney.

The governors of the hospital had always taken the view that St Luke's was a hospital and not a private lunatic asylum and as such it was not affected by any of the Lunacy Acts. However, by an Act passed in 1841 they became liable to visitation by the Metropolitan Commissioners appointed by the Home Secretary and, in 1845, an Act created a permanent commission and authorised the visitation of all institutions. The reports of the commissioners were on the whole favourable and helpful, although they were inclined to put forward counsels of perfection. In a report on the hospital in 1855, the commissioners expressed the opinion that the site of St Luke's, in what was now a very built-up area, and the appearance of the building, both inside and out, made it desirable that the governors consider moving to a new site and building. The governors rejected the recommendations on the grounds that, even if St Luke's did move further out to a more rural setting, an asylum would still be required in central London. The terms of their lease and the inadequacy of funds available, also made any move at that time impossible.

The subject of a move to a new site was to be raised on a further two occasions over the next 30 years but nothing came of the proposals. In 1875 Arthur Powell, who by then had been a member of the general committee for 34 years, was elected a vice-president, and in 1887 he was appointed treasurer. He was only to remain treasurer for three years but by then he was 70 years of age. In accepting his resignation in 1890 the general committee expressed their

... sense of the sincere gratification it has been to them to see him in that position even for a short time, they also desire to place a record of their appreciation of the very valuable services he has personally rendered over a period of 53 years [since he became a Governor] during which time he has ever taken the most active interest in everything pertaining to the hospital's welfare and your Committee have now pleasure in making expression of their warmest thanks to Mr Powell for his splendid and assiduous work.[4]

Arthur Powell died four years later in 1894. He had been the senior partner in Messrs James Powell and Sons glassworks at Whitefriars. In addition to his work with St Luke's, he was also a governor of St Bartholomew's Hospital and Christ's Hospital and a member of the council of Bradfield College. He was a JP and Commissioner of Taxes for Surrey. The link with the Powell family in the administration of the hospital was to continue as, in 1891, Arthur Crofts Powell, Arthur's son, had been elected to the general committee, and in 1896 he was made a vice-president.

It was during the years 1891–1894 that considerable improvements were carried out in the interior of the hospital. Better accommodation was provided for the staff. The wards were made lighter and less gloomy by the removal of the old and obsolete windows. All this was at considerable cost to the general fund, but much still remained to be done by the turn of the century. They wanted to instal electric light throughout the hospital and to have a modern heating plant as well.

In February 1901, Arthur Crofts Powell was elected as treasurer, an office he was to hold for 23 years and during which he was to be at the forefront of major changes to the charity and hospital. If St Luke's were to move from the Old Street site, an important consideration would always be the attitude of St Bartholomew's Hospital towards the termination of the lease. In 1903 there began long drawn-out negotiations which continued for 11 years before, in 1914, the governing bodies were able to reach agreement over the division of the proceeds from any sale of the lease of the Old Street site. Although no sale took place in 1914, the agreement, in the words of the General Committee 'greatly facilitated the business of selling the property to the Bank of England in 1916'.

Arthur Crofts Powell was the principal negotiator on behalf of St Luke's in all the meetings and exchanges with St Bartholomew's and the Corporation of London during this period. As soon as it became clear that the sale of the site to the Bank of England for their new printing works would take place, no further applications for admission to the hospital took place and the numbers in St Luke's were gradually reduced. All remaining in the hospital at the end of 1916 were either discharged to their homes or transferred to other institutions.

Following alterations to the buildings, the hospital became the St Luke's Printing Works of the Bank of England and remained so for 40 years. However, in the early 1950s, the need for more space resulted in the Bank of England building a new printing works on a 'greenfield' site at Debden near Loughton in Essex. The move from Old Street to Debden was completed in October 1956 and a few years later the Old Street site was redeveloped with council housing for the London Borough of Islington and is today known as the St Luke's Estate.

Links with the Middlesex Hospital

In 1917 there was no possibility of building a third St Luke's Hospital. The war was to continue for another 21 months and the shortage of materials and labour made it necessary to defer any thought of building operations. The future form of the charity therefore came under consideration. In 1922 it was suggested that a psychiatric unit should be instituted by St Luke's, in co-operation with a general hospital. The proposal was accepted in principle and Arthur Crofts Powell was authorised to approach the authorities of the Middlesex Hospital. The result was a formal agreement between the two hospitals under which St Luke's would meet the costs of establishing and maintaining six beds at the Middlesex as part of their neurological clinic, together with assistance with the out-patient work.

At the end of 1924 Mr Arthur Crofts Powell decided that he would not seek re-election as treasurer. He was now over 80 years old and had been treasurer for 23 and a governor for 38 years. The court and committee accepted his resignation with great regret and warm thanks for the work he had done at St Luke's. He was the fourth member of his family to hold this office and the policy of St Luke's Hospital had been guided and its finances guarded by a Powell during 76 years of the 174 years of its existence. The continuous link with the Powell family was, however, not broken. In 1915 Arthur Marriot Powell, Arthur Crofts Powell's son, had been elected to the general committee.

Woodside

In 1925 St Luke's again began to look seriously at establishing a new hospital on a site a little further from the centre of London. In 1926 the Committee reported favourably on a site near Muswell Hill. The site comprised two large villas next to each other, where the freehold was owned by the Ecclesiastical Commissioners, and a third house, where the tenant would sell if he could remain in the house for seven years. The three houses were next to one another and were the only residences in Woodside Avenue. Together they had a frontage of 220 yards on this road, with attractive gardens in an area totalling altogether six acres. Plans were drawn up for the conversion of the buildings into a hospital and building began in May 1928 and the Woodside Hospital was completed, furnished and equipped ready for the formal opening ceremony soon after the middle of 1930.

When the Old Street site was sold and St Luke's as a hospital ceased temporarily to exist, the thoughts of the governing body and their advisers turned towards those sufferers whose nerves were sick but who were not, as a rule, treated in a general hospital. On the other hand if they were sent to a mental hospital and had to associate with the patients there, the surroundings might well increase the mental strain and possibly aggravate their illness. The outcome of such thoughts was the experiment made in collaboration with the Middlesex Hospital. The establishment of the Woodside Nerve Hospital was a further step in this direction. Woodside made steady, if unadvertised, progress and the number of patients at any one time between 1935–1940 was 44. In 1938 the agreement with the Middlesex was terminated to allow resources to be concentrated on Woodside.

During the War Woodside received patients from each of the three armed Services, who had suffered from mental illness during the active campaigns.

In 1945 the future of St Luke's and Woodside again became a matter of discussion. For many years the general committee had looked at the possibility of St Luke's becoming a teaching hospital in psychological medicine. The impending introduction of a national health service, and the position of St Luke's-Woodside in this service, also needed to be considered. In 1946 it was suggested that the major teaching hospitals would have specialist hospitals linked to them and would thus become teaching groups. The governors of St Luke's approached the Middlesex Hospital with a proposal for amalgamation, and in July 1948 the amalgamation was completed and became fully operative. St Luke's, as a separate entity, ceased to exist and became the St Luke's-Woodside Branch of the Middlesex Hospital.

The link with the Powell family had continued with the opening of Woodside and Arthur Marriot Powell had been elected a vice-president in 1943. At the meeting of the court of governors in June 1948 the following statement was minuted:

As this is the last meeting to be held by the General Court of Governors while St Luke's Hospital has a separate and independent existence which has endured for 198 years all those present signed their names.[5]

Arthur Marriot Powell's signature appears among them.

It was agreed that the St Luke's-Woodside Hospital house committee would continue and a number of former governors of St Luke's remained members, including Powell. However, he resigned in October 1950 due to ill health and died in December. The house committee reported his death at their meeting on 12 December and the chairman noted that Mr Powell had been a member of the house committee for over 40 years and that his family had been connected with the hospital for over 200 years (strictly slightly less).

The hospital owed its inception, in 1750, to the humanitarian feelings of six City gentlemen. It did not derive from any monastic foundation nor from any single benefactor, but from plain well-to-do city merchants.[6] St Luke's and the Powell family have contributed much to both charity and medical progress. Today St Luke's-Woodside Hospital continues to serve the community, with over one hundred in-patients, and is part of the Camden and Islington Mental Health NHS Trust.

REFERENCES

1. French, C N, *The Story of St Luke's Hospital 1750–1948*, (1951), on which much of this chapter is based.
2. St Luke's-Woodside Hospital Archives, *General Committee Minute Book 1783*.
3. St Luke's-Woodside Hospital Archives, *Book of Rules of St Luke's Hospital and List of Governors for 1830*.
4. St Luke's-Woodside Hospital Archives, *General Committee Minute Book 1890*.
5. St Luke's-Woodside Hospital Archives, *General Court Minute Book 1948*.
6. French, C N, *The Story of St Luke's Hospital 1750–1948* (1951).

6

East Horndon, Essex

In 1901, shortly after the siege of Mafeking and its successful defence by General Robert Baden Powell, an article appeared in the *Home Counties Magazine,* illustrating the connection of Baden Powell's family with the parish of East Horndon in south Essex. The author of the memoir, Peter G Laurie, provided some details of the Powell pedigree from the time that the first David Powell travelled from Suffolk to London in 1712 to become an apprentice to a salter. The following extracts from the memoir refer directly to the link with East Horndon.

Very few, if any, of the residents of the parish of East Horndon, in Essex, have any idea of the association existing between the little hamlet of Herongate and the gallant and popular General, commonly called 'B-P', the heroic defender of Mafeking.

The Rev Harry Powell was the fourth surviving son, born on 20 June 1771 – 'at five minutes after eleven in the morning', according to the family Bible – was destined for the Church. On 12 July he was baptised at Homerton, his father and mother, David and Laetitia Powell, and his uncle Mr Thomas Powell, being sponsors on the occasion. He subsequently graduated, in 1793, at Trinity Hall, Cambridge, and was instituted to the living of East Horndon in 1795. On 6 July 1812, he married Anne, daughter of the Rev James Birch, of Corringham in Essex, by whom he had an only daughter, who did not survive, and who upon the theory that unbaptised infants should be buried 'between earth and Heaven', is said to have been deposited in a recess in the church wall adjacent to the north door, which has for many years been closed [Plate 29]. The Rev Harry Powell was a zealous and typical clergyman.

The old rectory, at that time, was in a state of hopeless dilapidation – it has since been turned into labourers' cottages – but the ancient chimney corners still exist [in 1901] and the remains of the old panelling may be traced through successive layers of paper and paint. The Rev Harry Powell purchased, and considerably improved and added to, a property in the parish, upon which he resided during his incumbency; and it is said he constructed at his own expense a good gravel path skirting the road and common, and passing at intervals through his own grounds, leading from the village to the church, and which he kept up at his own sole charge. By a singular fatality he was one day found in a dying state in his own meadow upon this very path, and being carried to his house he died shortly afterwards. His death took place on 1 February 1831, in the sixtieth year of his age, and he is buried in a vault in the chancel of East Horndon Church. The tablet to his memory in the old church speaks appreciatively of 'his life of primitive simplicity, spent in an humble endeavour to serve his Heavenly Master by a sincere and unremitting attention to all the duties of a Christian Minister', and alludes to the circumstance of his being 'suddenly called to his great account'. The Rev Harry Powell was the great uncle of General Robert Baden Powell.

His wife survived him many years, and, dying at St Leonards on 5 November 1869 is buried in the parish of Beauchamp Roding, near Ongar. Mrs Powell's niece, Juliana Laetitia Birch, married the Rev Edward H Landon, curate of the parish, and upon her marriage,

Rev Harry Powell (1771–1831)

Mr John Clark Powell, the Rev Harry Powell's eldest brother, settled upon her a little property in the parish of Ingrave, now known as the Manor House.

The Rev Harry Powell's mother, Laetitia, also died at East Horndon on 27 April 1801 while on a visit to her son, and is buried close to the altar rails in the church. A tablet to her memory on the chancel wall refers to her 'fourteen children, of whom five sons and five daughters survived and who bear the strongest testimony to the exemplary care which for nearly 40 years she took of her numerous family and are now the greatest comfort of her afflicted surviving Husband'.

Besides the tombs of Laetitia and the Rev Harry Powell in East Horndon Church, there is a large square altar-tomb in the churchyard to the memory of Mr John Powell, a wealthy wine merchant, of Millman Street, Holborn, in London, a cousin of the Rev Harry Powell, who died in 1799 at the age of 53.

Laurie concludes that 'we may profit by their good example and feel a sense of pride in the association of the Powell family with the parish of East Horndon in bygone times'.

The Church of All Saints at East Horndon needs to be mentioned in its own right. It stands on high ground, overlooking the Thames valley, however, for the past 70 years it has been isolated from the village by the London to Southend arterial road. The church is built almost entirely of brick and dates from the fifteenth and sixteenth centuries and the interior has several interesting and unusual features. East Horndon has been associated with the descendants of Sir John Tyrell, Speaker of the House of Commons, who died in 1437. It was his son, Thomas, who rebuilt the church.

The church has suffered much from decay and vandalism over many centuries, and by the 1890s was reported to be ruinous and 'will soon be hardly safe to worship in'. In 1898 the church was closed for worship on account of its dangerous condition, but after restoration, was reopened 10 years later. In the twentieth century the church was again allowed to decay and also suffered in 1944 when a bomb exploded close to it, destroying most of the glass and weakening the general structure of the building.

In 1970 a campaign to save the church was organised. The church was declared redundant in November 1970 but in May 1972 was vested in the Redundant Churches Fund scheme. Active local support through the All Saints Society resulted in a major programme of restoration, most of which was completed by the end of 1973. The church has since been used for concerts, exhibitions and the occasional service. In 1977 the monuments to the Powell family were reported to still be in place,[1] but the isolated position of the church continues to put it at risk to vandalism. The church is today in the care of the Churches Conservation Trust (Plate 28).

The Powell family scrapbooks[2] also contain the originals of a number of letters from the Rev Harry Powell to his brother James. They show that Harry's life was somewhat different from those of his brothers who were living near London and worked in the family business in the City. However, as we shall see, Harry still had a personal interest in the wine trade.

The first letter is undated but was probably written between 1810–1820. It is postmarked 'Brentwood' and is addressed to James Powell Esq at Carey Street, London:

Dear James

A story they say never loses by telling and I hope and trust this is true in the present case in the fullest extent of many of the words, for the reports of London disturbances which have reached this village are very uncomfortably alarming. I write therefore to request that none of the family who are inclined to make use of the premises here will wait for an invitation but come at once.

Yours Ever

Harry Powell

Heron Gate
Thursday

The second letter was sent to James Powell in 1815 and followed the birth of James and Catharine's daughter Mary Elizabeth (I have omitted the last paragraph):

Heron Gate, July 11 1815

Dear James

Accept our congratulations and hearty good wishes on the late addition to your circle. A feeling in which we shall ere long I trust more completely sympathise than ever, for though I have always felt a lively satisfaction in the increasing comforts of my best friends, the situation of my dear wife has roused feelings in my mind to which I must own myself hitherto almost a stranger and shewn me Duties which begin to make [me] very seriously anxious [Harry's wife Anne had recently become pregnant]. These thoughts it is probable are such as occur to every one whose attention is newly called to the subject, yet it is no small comfort to have so many friends around who are acquainted with the road I am to travel and to whom I can refer for advice.

Your affectionate brother

Harry Powell

A letter sent in 1816 includes a postscript which may suggest that Harry Powell was not as well off as his City brothers:

Heron Gate, Jan 12 1816

Dear James

We are much concerned to hear so sad an account of your good wife and her little ones and sincerely hope you will very soon be able to make a very different report of them which we shall be exceedingly glad to hear either at first or second hand as best suits the convenience of any Hackney Correspondents. We are I thank God going on well here and I have at length something like a glimpse of the end of my poor Anne's tedious confinement. The Dr talks of but ten days more. These afflictions may well serve to endear our wives to us if it were but as practical lessons of passive courage of which men would otherwise know little or nothing. Pray assure sister Catharine of sister Anne's most affectionate good wishes as with and those of yours.

Yours truly

Harry Powell

PS This morning's Waggon brings up two dozen empty bottles directed as usual to be called for and I hope it will not be very long [before] I settle accounts with you for the remaining full [amount].

The extracts from the final letter, written in 1819, concern James Powell's son, James Cotton, who was staying with his uncle Harry, and includes another postscript seeking 'supplies' from the wine merchant:

Heron Gate, Jan 1, 1819

Dear James

We are heartily concerned to hear you continue to give so indifferent an account but hope of poor sister James [this may refer to his wife] though we cannot but hope that Dr Sim's last suggestion may go far to relieve your most painful anxiety. Pray give our kind love to her and assure her of our best good wishes. We are all highly pleased with the good humoured cheerfulness and orderly pleasing manners of your Boy [James Cotton Powell], they reflect the highest credit upon somebody and if he goes on as well as he has begun will richly repay all the pains that have been taken with him. He takes me back every now and then to Brompton and the year 1784. He is I think a very respectable Latin scholar for his age [10 years]. We have matched him with a companion just older than him in age and attainments. PS When the weather will allow it, send me a gallon of Tent [sacramental] wine and fill the hamper up with Sherry. Let us hear from you soon. [My] wife says she is out of Tea, therefore you [could] if you please put 6 lbs of Twinings Tea into a hamper of old Port.

Your affectionate brother

Harry Powell

Another postscript to the life of the Rev Harry Powell occurred in 1870 when a suit in the Chancery Court was instituted by the Powell family. This friendly though expensive litigation arose on an ambiguous expression in the will of Harry Powell, as to the disposal of his property after his widow's death, in 1869. David Powell acted as plaintiff and Arthur Powell as defendant. The court required affidavits to be sworn to prove all the descendants of David Powell and Laetitia Clark from their marriage in 1761 and this was no doubt of value to Edgar Powell in 1891, when he published the genealogy of the family. Judgment was given in 1873.[3]

REFERENCES

1. Starr, C, *East Horndon Church: A History and Guide* (1977).
2. Vestry House Museum, Powell Family Scrapbooks, vol 4.
3. *Ibid.*

7

Nathanael Powell

Shore Place, Hackney

Nathanael Powell was one of eight children born to James and Catharine Powell. He was the third eldest son, and was born at Shore Place in Hackney on 15 October 1813. Nathanael described Shore Place as his father's 'country house'. James Powell's 'town house' was, until 1839, in Carey Street, behind the Law Courts. This also served as the offices, on the ground floor, for the family wine merchant's business. Shore Place lay between Well Street and Victoria Park Road and was a large detached, rambling house, with walled garden and paddock, stables, fruit rooms and cow house. The paddock was large enough for archery.

Catharine Powell was the centre of the large family's life and, with the assistance of a succession of governesses, looked after their early education. The whole family attended church twice every Sunday, notes were made on the sermons, and an extra sermon was read at home in the evening by Nathanael's father or an elder brother. Powell's sisters were entirely educated at home. Masters for singing, pianoforte and harp, and for dancing were called in to supplement the presiding governess. The only outdoor pursuits for young ladies were walking, riding, 'bowles' and archery.

In 1822, at the age of nine, Nathanael was sent as a boarder to Archbishop Harsnett's Grammar School at Chigwell, Essex [now known as Chigwell School]. In 1629 the Archbishop of York, who had been born at Colchester, and had become Vicar of Chigwell, founded, built and suitably endowed two schools at Chigwell. The schools were designed – one for the reading of the 'Latin and Greek tongues', the other that the children might be taught to 'Read, Write, Cypher, and cast Accounts, and to learn their Accidence'.[1] Nathanael's two elder brothers, James Cotton and Arthur, had preceded him at Chigwell and his younger brother John Cotton was to follow him. His cousin George, son of David and Grizell Powell of Loughton, also attended the school from 1827.

Life at the school was rough, sanitary arrangements were primitive and the yard pump played an important part in the morning toilet. Nathanael did not remember learning any Greek, and there was no natural science. No games were regularly organised but casual games of single-wicket cricket and football were played. The pupils swam in a shallow and muddy hole in the nearby River Roding. In his last year at Chigwell, Nathanael wrote to his father on 9 June 1829:

I have now the very pleasant task to inform you of the near approach of our midsummer vacation which is fixed to commence on Saturday twentieth of this month. I trust that you will find us both [his younger brother John was by now at the school] much improved in our studies as we have endeavoured to merit your approbation. Dr and Mrs Burford [the Headmaster and his wife] desire their compliments. John unites with me our best love to Mamma, our brothers and sisters.

Believe me,
My dear father,
Your dutiful son,
Nathanael Powell.[2]

Later in his life, Nathanael was to play an important role in the development of the school. After leaving Chigwell, Nathanael went to a private tutor in Northamptonshire. The tutor was probably his uncle, the Rev Thomas Sikes, the Rector of Guilsborough, who had married Susanna Powell, a sister of Nathanael's father. The year that he spent at Guilsborough was 'quiet and uneventful, we spent much time in making electrical apparatus out of bottles and telescopes with cardboard tubes'. On his return home, Nathanael, at the age of 17, joined his father in the wine merchant's business.

The distance from Shore Place to Carey Street was about four miles, and the daily journey to and from business was made either on foot or horseback. Powell, in a letter to his son Harry James, in August 1892, recounts his early life and comments that:

Business was a different process [in 1830] to that of today. My father impressed upon me that the main object was to make friends, and that money-making was a necessary but unfortunate incident. Customers' calls frequently extended into long visitations and involved much tasting of wine and a solid midday meal. The wine merchant often became the confidant and adviser on many subjects besides port, claret and madeira. The hours of business were rather indefinite, and were regulated more by the work to be done than by the hands of the clock. Correspondence and book-keeping were often resumed after supper and carried on till nine or ten at night.

Visits to the Theatre were events of sufficient rarity to be recorded in my diary. In the years 1831-32 are the following entries: 'Dined at Serl's Coffee House at 5/- per head, went to the Olympic: saw "My Eleventh Day" and "Olympic Devils": Liston and Madden Ventris acting'. 'At Covent Garden. Saw Fanny Kemble as Lady Macbeth.' 'Paganini's concert, terrible squeeze, very hot.'

At this time Nathanael also attended lectures at the newly opened King's College in the Strand. The subjects included zoology, geology and natural history, in which he was to maintain an interest through his membership of the Essex Archaeological Society and Essex Field Club.

Bloomsbury and Walthamstow

In August 1838 Nathanael married his cousin, Agnes, at St Nicholas Church, Loughton. Agnes was the seventh daughter of David Powell of Bench House, Loughton. Their first home was in Torrington Square in Bloomsbury where they lived for seven years and the first three of their 13 children were born. In 1845 they moved to Grove House in Grove Lane [Road], Walthamstow, Essex.

Grove House was a large mansion built in the latter part of the eighteenth century and the grounds around it were bounded by the present Beulah Road and Beulah Path, almost as far as Maynard Road. It was a three storeyed building, somewhat classical in style, and was considered one of the best built houses in Walthamstow.[3] It contained:

Four best bedchambers of large dimensions, four servants rooms, dressing room, school room, entrance hall, dining room 23 feet by 18 feet, drawing room 26 feet by 18 feet 6 inches, library and store room, excellent attached and detached offices, including butler's pantry, kitchen, larder, wine, beer and coal cellars, extensive yard, brewhouse, laundry, stabling for five horses, double coach houses and harness room.[4]

Another five of their children were born at Walthamstow, but their son Herbert Nathanael, who had been born at Torrington Square, was to die of enteritis at the age of nine while at Forest School, and Robert Arthur died in infancy in 1848. The 1851 Census shows Nathanael and Agnes living in

Grove House, Walthamstow, Essex, in 1885

Grove Lane with three daughters, Alice, Maria and Janette, together with six servants. It is not clear precisely when Nathanael and his family left Grove House but it may have been in about 1854, when they moved to Bedford House in Tavistock Square, near to their old house in Torrington Square. A neighbour at Bedford House was Charles Dickens. It is possible that Powell had a lease on Bedford House and treated it as his 'town house', for in 1855 he purchased a house at Buckhurst Hill, Essex, which he named 'Luctons'. They remained at Luctons for the rest of their lives and the last five of their children were born there.

Work in the community

Apart from his work in the family wine business, Nathanael had in 1834 become involved in the glassworks at Whitefriars that his father had purchased in that year, 'in order that his three sons should have sufficient occupation'. How James and his sons and grandson, Harry James Powell, developed Whitefriars is described in the next chapter. However, during the second half of the nineteenth century Nathanael was to devote much time to work in the community.

In 1857 he became a member of the committee of King's College Hospital, which at that time was in Portugal Street, just north of the Strand. During the early years of his connection with the hospital he helped to introduce a new system of nursing, using for the first time female nurses. He also came to know and support the work of Dr Joseph Lister, who lived at Upton, four or five miles from Powell's house at Walthamstow. Nathanael was appointed a vice-president of the hospital in 1890. He was of course following several generations of Powells in this charitable work for the medical profession.

In 1861 Nathanael was appointed a JP for the County of Essex and sat at Stratford and Ilford, which were part of the Becontree Division. This could take up two days of each week. In 1869 he was appointed a Deputy Lieutenant for Essex. He became a visitor of the County Asylum and also of HM Prison at Chelmsford. In 1864 he joined the Committee of the SPCK and became one of its treasurers.

Chigwell School

Nearer to his home at Buckhurst Hill, he renewed his contact with Chigwell School. In 1856 he was appointed a governor of the school and in 1862 a committee of governors, consisting of the Rev J Smith, the Rev W S H

Meadows, Major Suart and Nathanael Powell, was appointed 'to consider and report on the present condition of the schools, and the means by which their usefulness to the neighbourhood might be increased'. This came at a time shortly after the passing of the Endowed Schools Act when most anciently endowed schools had effectively to be refounded.

One key proposal was the separation of the Grammar School from the English (National) School. However, it was not until 1867 that a new scheme for the management of the school was agreed by the Charity Commissioners. The Grammar School was to occupy the old buildings, and a new building for the National School, funded in part by public subscription, was to be built on a site in Harsnett's garden. Additions were made to the Grammar School buildings in 1868 and 1871, and in 1872 a chapel was erected. In 1876 a new classroom was urgently needed and thanks to the generosity of two governors, one of whom was Nathanael Powell, this was built. Nathanael became chairman of the school governors in 1874 and eventually by special dispensation of the Charity Commissioners, an honorary governor from 1901 until his death in 1906.

In reviewing Powell's contribution to the School, *The Chigwellian Magazine* said:

With John Smith (Rector of Buckhurst Hill) and William Swainson Suart (of the Bowls) the name of Nathanael Powell goes down to posterity as the Triumvirate who rescued the School from the position of worthless obscurity into which it had fallen in 1865, and started it on its present career of success. His purse strings were always untied in response to any appeal for the needs of the School.[5]

Nathanael was also one of the managers of St John's National School at Buckhurst Hill, which a schools inspector stated at the time was what he regarded as a model elementary school.

A village hospital in Knighton Lane was founded in 1869 by subscription on the initiative of Dr C H Livingstone and Nathanael Powell and grew into an important institution serving a large area.

Nathanael Powell (1813–1906)

Political allegiances

After the passing of the Local Government Act of 1888, Powell was elected an alderman of Essex County Council. He was a firm supporter of Conservative principles but although strongly attached to his party a contemporary writer commented that he 'never allows himself to be betrayed into the use of language calculated to hurt the feelings of his most sensitive opponents, and in this respect it may be said that he belongs to a school of politicians which is not as strongly represented in the world as it should be'.

In 1880 he was elected founder chairman of the Chingford Conservative Association having campaigned for Sir H J Selwyn-Ibbetson, who was returned as Member in May 1880. He often hosted the Party's summer fete in the grounds of Luctons at Buckhurst Hill. He resigned from the County Council in 1896 on account of his age; he was by then 83 years old.

Luctons

Nathanael and Agnes Powell had moved to Luctons in 1855. The house was originally a small white cottage standing on 'the common': a small piece of forest waste, near the Roebuck Inn. It was built in the early part of the seventeenth century. The Powells added to it at two different periods. The larger portion was built in about 1860. Nathanael built up a considerable estate around Luctons, extending along the High Road from Roebuck Lane to Russell Road. Further land on the east side of Roebuck Lane brought this part of the estate to 20 acres. On the west side of the High Road the estate included land from Ardmore Lane northwards, crossing the parish boundary with Loughton to Manor Road. This land extended westwards but not as far as the Epping New Road.

Much of this land was part of Epping Forest and Powell appears to have purchased and subsequently enclosed it. In the 1850s the enclosure of Epping Forest, by the Lords of the Manors and other landowners, had led to a great outcry and the appointment of the Epping Forest Commission, which was ultimately to result in the Epping Forest Act of 1878 under which the Corporation of London became the owners and Conservators of the Forest. An arbitration was set up, under Sir Arthur Hobhouse, to decide which enclosures should be returned to the Forest, but before their work had been completed, disquiet led to the public taking action themselves to remove the fences. George Burney took a leading part in this action and a newspaper report of the time refers to:

The fences that were destroyed last week by Mr George Burney, Chairman of the Epping Forest Preservation Society, and his hundred followers, have in most cases been replaced.

The strong arm of the law has stretched out to prevent Mr Burney from committing any more of these outrageous acts, and he will appear before the Master of the Rolls today (Friday) to justify, if he can, his actions. Two, *ad interim,* injunctions were immediately applied for by G Borwick and N Powell Esq, which the Master of the Rolls granted, to restrain the defendants from doing further injury till the case has been before him.

Over 2,000 acres of the land that had been enclosed was put back into the Forest and this included Powell's land from the cricket field north to Manor Road.

We are fortunate that one of the daughters of Nathanael and Agnes made up scrapbooks of life at Luctons and the wider Powell family further afield. They consist of six volumes that have survived and now reside in the Archives Department of the London Borough of Waltham Forest at the Vestry House Museum. It is clear that Nathanael had been a founder member, if not founder, of the Buckhurst Hill Cricket Club in 1864. He had provided a ground for them opposite his house. This was originally enclosed forest land, but as we have seen, subsequent to the Epping Forest Act, it again became open forest land. The Club have continued to play at the ground with their landlord changing in 1879 to the Corporation of London, as the Conservators of Epping Forest. Powell became President of the Club and on occasion, during 'Cricket Week', he put out a team consisting entirely of members of the Powell family.

Buckhurst Hill, like most villages in England, celebrated national events, including in 1863 the marriage of the Prince of Wales (later Edward VII) and Princess Alexandra of Denmark. A dinner with 'pudding and ale' was provided for 100 of the deserving poor. Powell acted as Treasurer in organising the event. The Golden Jubilee of Queen Victoria in 1887 was celebrated in similar fashion.

It appears that horseracing took place over a course of 1½ miles on land behind Luctons. Programmes for 1859 refer to the Woodford & Loughton Stakes, the Tally Ho Stakes and the Ladies Plate. Admission to the Race Course for those on foot was 3d. Dinner was provided after the Races at 7 o'clock, no doubt at the Roebuck Inn.

In March 1867 Powell's daughter, Alice, produced the first edition of the 'Ben Buckhurst Hill Chronicle' which gave details of Powell family events. Alice, like her father, was exceptionally tall, over six feet.

A watercolour drawing of Luctons in 1872 (see Plate 30) was made by the Rev R C Caswall. His son, Alfred, married Nathanael's sister, Mary Elizabeth. Mr Caswall made sketches in colour of many events at Luctons, including members of the family acting in the theatrical performances that they put on at the house. The daughters often wrote the plays as well as performing in them.

Agnes Powell's time must have been fully taken up in looking after her

13 children. In 1888 an appeal was made to residents of Buckhurst Hill for donations to a golden wedding anniversary gift to Agnes and Nathanael. A local newspaper reported that 'the gift from the residents of Buckhurst Hill was a clock with chimes by Messrs Moore, in an oak case, and an illuminated album with the names of 554 subscribers'.

Agnes died in 1902. The *Woodford Times* in reporting the funeral commented that the Powells during a period of almost 50 years had exhibited an unceasing interest in all matters relating to the spiritual and material welfare of the parish. The erection of the new parish church of St John's was due, in a very great measure to the initiative of Mrs Powell.

Nathanael Powell died at Luctons in January 1906 after an active life well lived. He was in his ninety-third year but his health had been failing for some two years. An obituary in the *Essex Review* in April 1906 commented that he had 'spent his long life in the pursuit of philanthropy'. He had been a partner in Whitefriars glassworks at the height of its reputation and, through his work in the community and active membership of the church, he had become known and respected throughout the county. He had spent little on himself and accumulated no great fortune. Nathanael was buried in the family vault in the churchyard at St John's, Buckhurst Hill.

Within four years of his death, Luctons had been sold and demolished and the surrounding land developed for housing.

Harry James Powell

Harry James Powell was born in Walthamstow in 1853 and was Nathanael's eldest surviving son. He was educated at Rugby and Trinity College, Oxford, and in 1875 joined the Whitefriars glass factory where he was to play an important part in the development of glass production in England. This part of his life is described in the next chapter. In January 1875 he married Emma Suart, daughter of Major Suart of The Bowles, Chigwell, whom we have already come across as one of the triumvirate of Governors of Chigwell School who restored it to success in the 1870s. A daughter, Muriel, was born later in 1875 while Harry and Emma were living at the glassworks. In the early 1880s they lived at the White House in Loughton, a mile or so from Luctons.

Outside his business life, Harry James Powell was in January 1889 elected to the London County Council as the member for Dulwich, to where they had moved. He followed in his father's footsteps and was a member of the Committee of Management of King's College Hospital from 1885–1887.

Harry James Powell (1853–1922)

The Powell daughters

All the Powell daughters who lived at Buckhurst Hill involved themselves in the life of the local community. Janette, who was probably the daughter who put the scrapbooks together, was for many years Sunday School Superintendent, a post from which she retired in 1901. In her later years she lived at Hawstead, a mansion built by Nathanael on the west side of the High Road, opposite Luctons. The name of course came from the hamlet in Suffolk from which the Powells came to London in the early eighteenth century. A block of flats replaced the mansion in the 1970s but still perpetuates the name.

Beatrice Pryor Powell was the musical member of the family. In 1882 she organised a series of 'Pleasant Evenings' at the Roebuck Hall where she was the soprano soloist. In later life she became a local magistrate. She lived in a house called Southfleet, which had been built in the grounds of Luctons shortly before Nathanael's death. She later moved to Hawstead.

Rachel Clark Powell was born in 1864 and was the youngest of the Powell daughters. A talented amateur actress and artist, she was known as 'Pretty Toes' to the family. In 1905 it was reported that Buckhurst Hill Hall [now the Library] was transformed into a Japanese Tea House by Rachel Powell for a novel entertainment. The proceeds were given to the Shoe Club and Penny Bank. In the following year she ran a Gypsy Camp to raise more funds for the same charity. She had a deep interest in the work of the Girls' Friendly Society and in the work of St Stephen's Church in Buckhurst Hill. A brass memorial in St Stephen's commemorates her work with the children of that church.

Edmund Nathanael Powell,
Bishop of Mashonaland

Edmund Nathanael Powell was the fifth son of Nathanael and Agnes, and was born in 1859. He was educated at Winchester and Trinity College, Oxford, where he was more known as a sportsman than an academic. He entered the church and in June 1883 was appointed to a curacy at Chelmsford. In April 1887 he left St Mary's, Chelmsford, to work in the Beckton Mission Church of St Michael and All Angels. The church was bombed in 1941 and was not rebuilt.

He left Beckton in 1891 to become Perpetual Curate of St Stephen's, Upton Park. Here he raised funds to extend the church and build a new chancel. Further extensions followed in 1896 bringing the total accommodation to 1,150. It is said to have been built largely with money subscribed by evangelical churchmen and conferred upon itself the distinction of being a memorial to Elizabeth Fry. It is clear that the parish was regarded as a mission field of especial importance. During Powell's incumbency over £20,000 were spent on purchasing sites and erecting mission churches. At one time he had six curates on his staff. In 1902 he was offered the living of St Thomas the Martyr at Brentwood but he declined, preferring to stay in Upton Park. He stayed at St Stephen's for a total of 15 years. It was by far the most remarkable part of his career. Upton Park had a rapidly developing population. He drew great numbers around him, won their affection and confidence and filled the great church to overflowing. In 1940 the church was wrecked by bombing, and after the war it was decided that it should not be rebuilt and the remains were demolished in 1954.

In 1908 Powell was appointed Bishop of Mashonaland. A grand farewell party was provided by the parishioners of St Stephen's and held at East Ham Town Hall. In November of that year Oxford University conferred an Honorary Doctorate of Divinity, as was their custom with all graduates appointed Bishop. He was consecrated Bishop at St George's Cathedral in Cape Town and enthroned in the Pro-Cathedral of St Mary and All Saints in Salisbury [Harare], Rhodesia [Zimbabwe] on 29 April 1908. The Diocese comprised the territories of Rhodesia and Bechuanaland with a population of 600,000 of whom less than 18,000 were English speaking. Powell was, however, to spend less than two years in Africa, before ill-health forced him to return to England.

After a period of recovery he was appointed to St Saviour's, Poplar, where he worked for several years before ill health again affected him. After a serious operation and recuperation he became vicar of Castle Hedingham in Essex. He remained there for four years but the country was not his sphere and he yearned for his former haunts in London-over-the-Border, and the great artisan populations he knew so well. He was appointed to St Columba's, Wanstead Slip, and was once more in his proper element. (St Columba's was merged in 1953 with St Margaret's in Woodhouse Road, Leytonstone.) Powell died in April 1929 and was buried in the family vault at St John's, Buckhurst Hill.[6] Anne Louisa Powell, one of Edmund Nathanael Powell's sisters, devoted her life to acting as her brother's companion and lived with him when he served at Beckton and in other parishes. She became Secretary of the [National] Girls Friendly Society which was founded in 1875 and by 1881 boasted 62,000 members.

The Church of St John the Baptist, Buckhurst Hill

Nathanael and Agnes Powell moved to Buckhurst Hill almost 20 years after the chapel of ease of St John the Baptist had been built. Agnes, before she married, lived at Bench House, Loughton, only a mile away at the foot of the hill. She and her mother, Grizell, had supported the building of the new church, which was then part of the parish of Chigwell. In 1838 Buckhurst Hill was constituted as a separate ecclesiastical district and in 1867 it became a separate parish.[7]

We have seen that all the members of the Powell family were active supporters of the church and it is therefore not surprising that the church benefited from their generosity, both while they were alive and as memorials to them after their deaths. Nathanael Powell had served as a churchwarden for 36 years until his retirement in 1893. In 1907, a year after Nathanael's death, a stained glass east window was erected in the church in his, and his wife's memory. The window was a gift from their children and other relations. In the same year a new pulpit was given in memory of Nathanael.

A sedilia and encaustic tiled floor had been given by the family in 1905 in memory of Rachel Powell, who had died at the relatively young age of 40 years. The Powell family's concern for children was reflected in the inscription on the fine Victorian Font given in 1865 by Agnes Powell. Nathanael also made a substantial donation in 1863–64 towards the cost of building an extension at the east end of the north aisle, specially for children. Some oak doors at the entrance to the nave were given in 1913, as a memorial to Janette Powell.[8]

REFERENCES

1. Swallow, R D, *Chigwell School Register* (1907).
2. Vestry House Museum, Powell Family Scrapbooks, vol 4, p 3.
3. Bosworth, G, *Houses in Walthamstow,* Walthamstow Antiquarian Society, Mono No 12 (1924).
4. Vestry House Museum, Pamphlet of House Sale in 1841.
5. Chigwell School, *The Chigwellian Magazine,* Shrove Tuesday (1906).
6. *Church Times*, 20 April 1929.
7. Powell, W R (Ed), *Victoria County History of Essex,* vol IV.
8. Gaunt Hunter, J, *Church and Community* (1987).

8

Whitefriars Glassworks

The flint-glass factory

The Whitefriars Glassworks was founded in about 1680 on a site between Fleet Street and the Thames, just east of the Temple, in the City of London. Originally the site housed the Monastery of the Carmelite Fathers, who were known as the White Friars. In choosing the site for a glassworks, the founder, William Davis, was no doubt influenced by ready access to the wharves from which to draw Newcastle coal, sand, clay and the other materials with which to make glass.

Early references to the glass factory appeared in *The Tatler* in 1710 and consisted of advertisements of 'all sorts of decanthers, drinking glasses and crewits, to be obtained wholesale or retail at the Flint Glassworks in White Fryars near the Temple'.[1]

The buildings at first were primitive, being little better than lofty sheds, to a great extent open to the street. The furnace cones were low and wide and sent out volumes of dense smoke. Work in the factory was primitive and tough, as is illustrated by a cutting from the *Whitehall Evening Post* of 1732:

Yesterday a Press Gang went into the glasshouse in White Fryars to press some of the men at work there, but they were no sooner got in but the [molten] metal was flung about 'em, and happy was he that could get out first, and in the hurrying out they ran over their officer, who was almost scalded to death.[2]

Ownership of the glassworks changed several times before James Powell acquired the business from William Holmes in 1834. By 1833 the number of licensed glasshouses in London had been reduced to three. Manufacturers had been driven out of the trade by a combination of competition from low priced provincial glass and the restrictive effects of the glass excise. From 1745 to 1845 all glass factories were subject to the payment of excise duty. The excise was a government tax levied on all manufactured glass and collected at the point of manufacture rather than the point of sale. It had been introduced on the grounds that glass was a 'luxury' and therefore suitable for taxation.

Excisemen were quartered on the premises and it was their duty to interfere with every manufacturing process. Failure to carry out any one of hundreds of petty regulations rendered the manufacturer liable to a heavy fine and he was entirely at the mercy of the supervising officers. It is a matter of surprise that any manufacturer should tolerate such interference or that any factory should have survived it. However, to Nathanael Powell it was all very interesting:

The business of wine and glass were worked together and for some years I divided my time between them. I can recollect no incident of interest in the wine business except that in 1848, at the time of the Chartist demonstrations, the wine cellars were securely barricaded for fear of riots and looting. The glass business with its many failures and occasional success was by far the most interesting.[3]

Stained glass windows

If James Powell and his initial partner, Arthur, his second son, were ignorant of glassmaking, they appear to have soon acquired an enthusiasm for the chemical composition of glass and experimented making different colours. Whitefriars was originally a table glass firm but in 1844 the factory introduced and patented a process of stamping small diamond shaped panes of glass, known as 'quarries', for church windows. This process also avoided the excise regulations that flint-glass works could not produce glass for windows either by blowing or rolling. Stamped quarries and coloured glasses led to a search for artists who were competent to make designs and drawings for windows. Help was obtained from Edward Burne-Jones, Ford Madox Brown, Edward Poynter, Henry Holliday and other young artists. The outstanding East windows at Waltham Abbey in Essex are based on designs by Burne-Jones and were installed in 1861.[4]

The Great Exhibition of 1851 marked the start of a period of success and expansion for Powells. The glassworks was improved and enlarged in 1856, 1862 and 1864 and the profits from 1838 to 1897 showed a healthy upward trend.

By 1851 the firm was being managed by the three brothers, Arthur, Nathanael and John. The most important development for the glassworks during the period 1851-1872 was the expansion of the window department, which was said to have doubled its sales by 1872. By 1870 Powells was firmly established in most architects' minds as one of the country's leading suppliers of high quality ecclesiastical stained glass.

Two of Arthur's sons, Arthur Crofts (1844-1929) and James Crofts (1847-1914), had also worked for the business since the mid 1860s, the latter at some time becoming responsible for the window department. Nathanael remained a partner until his death in 1906 but, according to his memoir, did not play an active part in the firm after the arrival of recruits from a younger generation and he was thus able to devote more time to his external work.

The stained glass department by the end of the century offered mural treatments, memorials and tiles as well as windows. An economical desire to prevent waste led to the development of the craft of mosaic. It had been the custom to scrap as useless all fragments of flint-glass contaminated with clay, but experiments proved that this waste glass, if ground to a fine powder and baked, yielded a solid, durable material with an eggshell surface for wall tiles and mosaic, and the range of colours was almost unlimited. This material was used in 1884 for a fine mosaic on the east wall of the Morning Chapel of St Paul's Cathedral. Sir William Richmond's mosaics in the choir and choir aisles of St Paul's were commenced in 1891 and, on their completion in 1896, were celebrated by a special Thanksgiving Service.[5]

In 1907, the Churchwardens of St John the Baptist Church at Loughton were granted a faculty to replace the existing three stained glass windows in the chancel with new ones to commemorate the Golden Jubilee of the Rector, John Whitaker Maitland. Subscriptions were invited to meet the cost, and four members of a committee formed to promote the idea, visited the glassworks of James Powell and Sons to discuss designs and cost. In addition to the windows, an alabaster retable was also proposed. No doubt the links with those members of the Powell family who lived at Loughton and Buckhurst Hill influenced the decision to approach Whitefriars. The glorious east window and retable remain today as memorials to both J W Maitland and the art of Whitefriars.[6]

Harry James Powell

Of all the members of the Powell family who were partners of James Powell & Sons or who worked at the factory, Nathanael's son, Harry James, was to achieve most in the development of the firm. As we have seen in an earlier chapter, Harry read chemistry at Oxford and his approach to glassmaking was that of a scientist and this informed all his work at the glassworks and elsewhere. It was fundamentally the reason he took up history and why he began designing glass.

Part of the firm's character certainly flowed from its ability to function as a jobbing glasshouse within a large urban economy, both supplying and responding to particular needs of its metropolitan customers. The character of London's export trade, the presence in London of a body of customers with wealth and taste, London's links with the continent and the opportunities for exhibiting glass that London provided: all these things affected what James Powell & Sons made.[7]

At the factory Harry James Powell's influence over his workmen was very great and by his training the works employed some of the best craftsmen in the country. Harry joined Whitefriars in 1873, became Works Manager in 1875, and remained in charge until 1919. He became junior partner in 1885. His notebooks underline not only his enquiring mind but also his ability for sheer hard work. Soon after joining the firm he not only read for a home study pass degree in law and history but also arranged to have photography lessons. Later, carrying on the family tradition, he devoted some of his energy to public life, serving on several London and national committees concerned with science and industry, technical education, education and art. In 1889, with the backing of the Conservatives, he was elected as a member for Dulwich on the first LCC. He became a governor of Dulwich College with the encouragement of Sidney Webb. In 1908 he was one of three manufacturers on the Board of Education Committee of Re-arrangement at the Victoria and Albert Museum which aimed to increase the usefulness of the museum to craftsmen and those with a practical interest in decorative arts. His wartime industrial activities were rewarded with a CBE in 1920 which he was persuaded reluctantly to accept.[8] He died in 1922.

In 1923 the factory moved out of London to Wealdstone. In 1952 G H Zeal Ltd, a manufacturer of clinical thermometers and an old customer of Powell's for its glass tubing, took a controlling interest in the firm. In the early 1970s the factory ceased making stained glass, but continued to suffer losses due to fierce foreign competition. In 1980 the factory was closed. Members of the Powell family had been involved with Whitefriars for almost 150 years.

Examples of stained glass and mosaics, by James Powell & Sons, in Essex, may be found in the following churches (these are the ones that I have checked, there are others):

Waltham Abbey	Abbey Church of Waltham Holy Cross and St Lawrence
Loughton	Church of St John the Baptist
Chigwell	St Mary's Church
Coopersale	St Alban's Church
High Beach	Holy Innocents' Church
Buckhurst Hill	St John's Church
Southend	All Saints Church; St John's Church
Leigh-on-Sea	Church of Our Lady of Lourdes
Great Warley	Church of St Mary the Virgin
Colchester	St Botolph's Church

REFERENCES

1. Powell, H J, *Glass-Making in England* (1923).
2. *Ibid.*
3. Powell, N, Letter to H J Powell (1892).
4. Powell, H J, *Glass-Making in England* (1923).
5. *Ibid.*
6. Essex Record Office, Notebook on commemoration of Rector's Jubilee, Ref. D/P 233/24/6.
7. Evans, W and others, *Whitefriars Glass, James Powell & Sons* (1995).
8. *Ibid.*

APPENDIX A – TABLE A: DAVID POWELL PEDIGREE FROM 1695

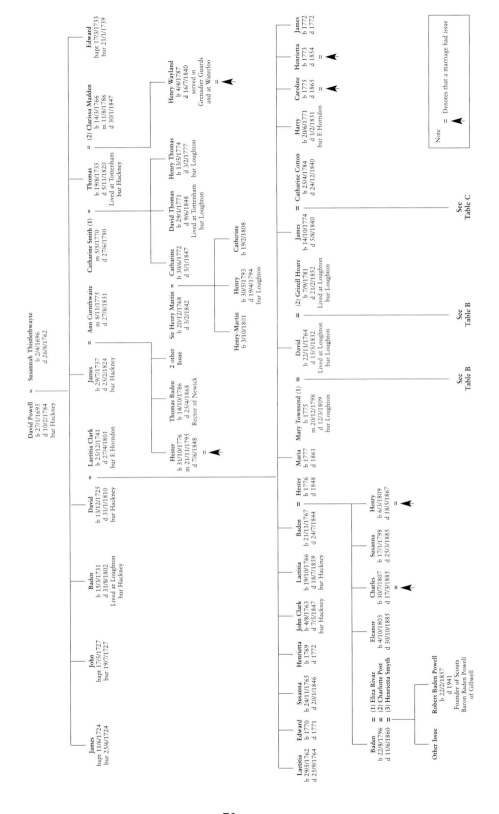

73

TABLE B: DAVID POWELL PEDIGREE FROM 1764

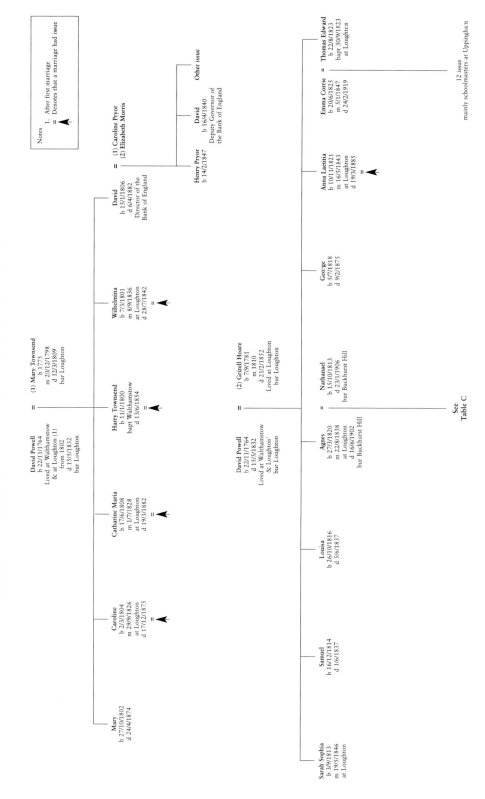

Notes   1.   After first marriage
         =   Denotes that a marriage had issue

David Powell
b 22/11/1764
Lived at Walthamstow
& at Loughton (1)
from 1802
d 15/5/1832
bur Loughton

=   (1) Mary Townsend
        b 1775
        m 20/12/1798
        d 12/3/1809
        bur Loughton

=   (1) Caroline Pryor
    (2) Elizabeth Morris

Mary
b 27/10/1802
d 24/4/1874

Caroline
b 2/3/1804
m 29/9/1826
at Loughton
d 17/12/1875
=

Catharine Maria
b 17/6/1808
m 1/7/1828
at Loughton
d 19/3/1882
=

Harry Townsend
b 11/1/1800
bapt Walthamstow
d 13/6/1854
=

Wilhelmina
b 7/3/1801
m 8/9/1836
at Loughton
d 28/7/1842
=

David
b 15/1/1806
d 6/4/1882
Director of the
Bank of England

Other issue

Henry Pryor
b 14/2/1847

David
b 16/4/1840
Deputy Governor of
the Bank of England

David Powell
b 22/11/1764
d 15/5/1832
Lived at Walthamstow
& Loughton¹
bur Loughton

=   (2) Grizell Hoare
        b 7/9/1781
        m 1810
        d 21/2/1852
        Lived at Loughton
        bur Loughton

Sarah Sophia
b 3/9/1813
m 19/5/1846
at Loughton

Samuel
b 16/12/1814
d 1/6/1837

Louisa
b 26/10/1816
d 5/6/1837

Agnes
b 27/3/1820
m 22/8/1838
at Loughton
d 16/6/1902
bur Buckhurst Hill
=

Nathanael
b 15/10/1813
d 23/1/1906
bur Buckhurst Hill

George
b 5/7/1818
d 9/2/1875

Anna Laetitia
b 10/11/1821
m 16/5/1843
at Loughton
d 19/3/1885
=

Emma Corrie
b 20/6/1825
m 5/1/1847
d 24/2/1919

Thomas Edward
b 22/8/1823
bapt 30/9/1823
at Loughton
=

12 issue
mainly schoolmasters at Uppingham

See
Table C

74

TABLE C: DAVID POWELL PEDIGREE FROM 1774

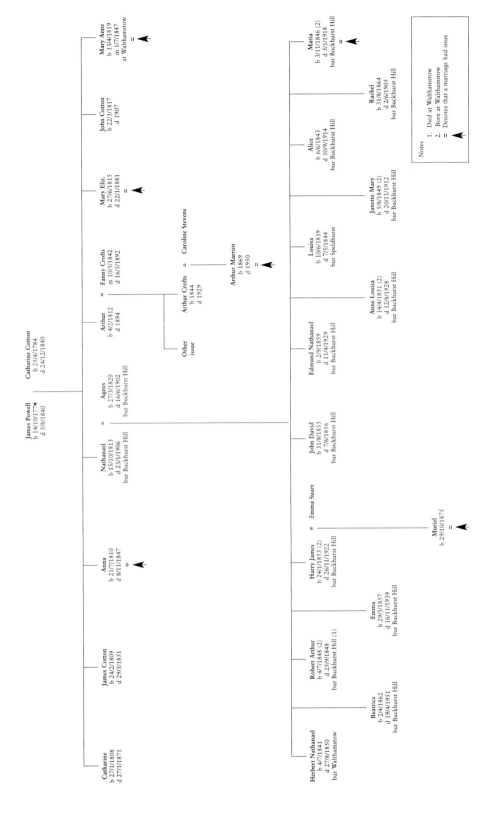

James Powell
b 14/10/1774 [1]
d 5/8/1840

=

Catharine Cotton
b 25/4/1784
d 24/12/1840

Catharine
b 27/1/1808
d 27/1/1871

James Cotton
b 24/2/1809
d 29/3/1851

Anna
b 21/7/1810
d 8/11/1847 ←

Nathanael
b 15/10/1813
d 23/1/1906
bur Buckhurst Hill

=

Agnes
b 27/3/1820
d 16/6/1902
bur Buckhurst Hill

Arthur
b 4/2/1812
d 1894

=

Fanny Crofts
m 10/5/1842
d 16/5/1892

Mary Eliz.
b 27/6/1815
d 22/1/1881 ←

John Cotton
b 22/3/1817
d 1907

Mary Anne
b 13/4/1819
m 17/1/1847
at Walthamstow ←

Arthur Crofts
b 1844
d 1929

=

Caroline Stevens

Arthur Marriot
b 1869
d 1950 ←

Other
issue

Herbert Nathanael
b 4/7/1841
d 25/9/1850
bur Walthamstow

Beatrice
b 2/4/1862
d 19/4/1951
bur Buckhurst Hill

Robert Arthur
b 4/7/1848 (2)
d 25/9/1848
bur Buckhurst Hill (1)

Emma
b 29/5/1857
d 16/1/1939
bur Buckhurst Hill

Harry James
b 24/1/1853 (2)
d 26/11/1922
bur Buckhurst Hill

=

Emma Suart

John David
b 31/8/1855
d 7/6/1856
bur Buckhurst Hill

Edmund Nathanael
b 29/1/1859
d 11/4/1929
bur Buckhurst Hill

Anne Louisa
b 14/4/1851 (2)
d 12/8/1928
bur Buckhurst Hill

Louisa
b 10/6/1839
d 7/5/1844
bur Speldhurst

Janette Mary
b 5/8/1849 (2)
d 20/11/1912
bur Buckhurst Hill

Alice
b 6/6/1843
d 30/9/1914
bur Buckhurst Hill

Rachel
b 31/8/1864
d 2/6/1905
bur Buckhurst Hill

Maria
b 3/11/1846 (2)
d 5/1/1918
bur Buckhurst Hill ←

Muriel
b 29/10/1875 =

Notes

1. Died at Walthamstow
2. Born at Walthamstow
= Denotes that a marriage had issue ←

75

APPENDIX B

David Thomas Powell (1771–1848) MSS held at the British Library and other institutions

British Library

Add MS 17436	Knights of the Order of St Michel (France).
Add MS 17438	Arms of the Knights of the Golden Fleece (2 vols).
Add MS 17439	Coats of arms of English families.
Add MS 17441	Genealogical quarterings of the descendants of the monarchs of England.
Add MS 17442	Order of St Esprit.
Add MS 17453	Arms with monumental inscriptions collected from parish Churches in England.
Add MS 17454	Pedigrees and arms of various families in England.
Add MS 17456	Topographical collections for Bedfordshire and Buckinghamshire.
Add MS 17457	Topographical collections for Berkshire.
Add MS 17458	Topographical collections for Cambridgeshire, Herefordshire and Hertfordshire.
Add MS 17459	Topographical collections for Devon and Dorset.
Add MS 17460	Topographical collections for Essex.
Add MS 17461	Pedigrees of Essex families.
Add MS 17462	Topographical collections for Leicestershire, Lincolnshire and Norfolk.
Add MS 17463	Topographical collections for Somerset.
Add MS 17694	Drawings of monuments in Westminster Abbey.
Add MS 17733	Topographical collections for Kent.
Add MS 19915	Topographical collections for Nottinghamshire and Derbyshire.
Add MS 20072	Order du Thoison D'Or, with arms and titles of sovereigns and knights 1429-1559.
Add MS 22505	David Thomas Powell personal catalogue of his collections and library.
Add MS 26677	Copy of a roll of arms of English families in the Ashmolean Library, Oxford, by D T Powell.

Egerton

MSS 2837–
2841

Volumes of correspondence with Sir Frederick Madden (1801–1873), who was appointed Head of the Manuscripts Department at the British Museum in 1837. There are some letters in the collection between D T Powell and Sir Frederick Madden.

Oxford University: Bodleian Library

MS top Oxon
b 256

Notes and drawings of Oxfordshire churches and buildings.

Lambeth Archives Department

n/k

Notes and drawings on Surrey churches.

Cardiff Central Library

n/k

Drawings of ecclesiastical buildings, Wales and borders.

Bath Central Library

Phillipps MS
29868

Notes on Somerset.

Northampton Central Library

n/k

Illustrated journal of visit to Northants.

West Yorkshire Archive Service

MSS 293–295

Yorkshire collections.

Counties visited by David Thomas Powell in his topographical survey of England and Wales

Buckinghamshire
Berkshire
Bedfordshire
Cambridgeshire
Dorset
Derbyshire
Essex
Gloucestershire
Hertfordshire
Hampshire
Huntingdonshire
Kent
Lancashire
Leicestershire
Lincolnshire
Middlesex
Norfolk
Nottinghamshire
Northamptonshire
Oxfordshire

Shropshire
Surrey
Sussex
Staffordshire
Suffolk
Somerset
Warwickshire
Wiltshire
Worcestershire
Yorkshire
WALES:
  Brecknockshire
  Carmarthenshire
  Radnorshire
  Denbighshire
  Glamorgan
  Herefordshire
  Montgomeryshire
  Pembrokeshire
  Monmouthshire

Map of the Powell Estate in Loughton
c 1850

(Based on a plan of the estate at the time of its sale in 1899)

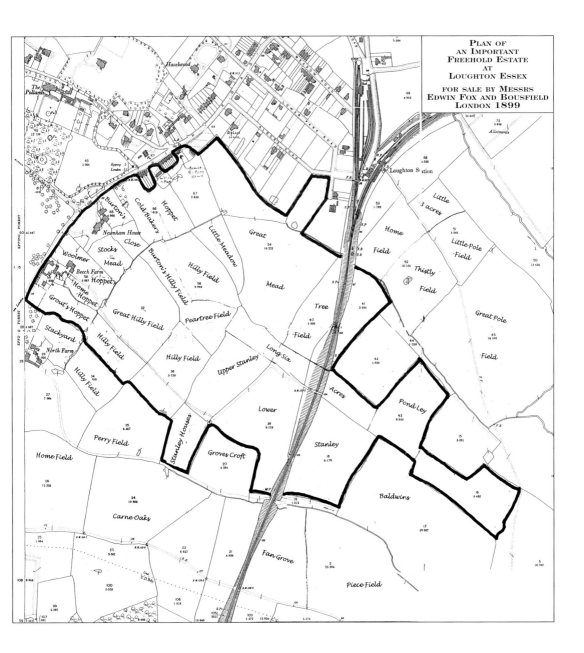

Index

Note: Members of the Powell family sharing the same forename
have been assigned a roman numeral in this index to help to make their
identification and their relationships clear. The abbreviation
qv (= 'which see') is used for some cross-references.